The Role of Analysis in
Regulatory Decisionmaking

The Role of Analysis in Regulatory Decisionmaking

The Case of Cable Television

Rolla Edward Park, Editor
Gary L. Christensen
William S. Comanor
John A. Dimling, Jr.
Kenneth R. Goodwin
Roger G. Noll
Bruce M. Owen
Douglas W. Webbink

Lexington Books
D.C. Heath and Company
Lexington, Massachusetts
Toronto   London

Library of Congress Cataloging in Publication Data
Main entry under title:

The Role of analysis in regulatory decision making.

"Outgrowth of a panel discussion at the meeting of the Western Economic
Association in August 1972."
  1. Community antenna television—Law and legislation—United States—
Addresses, essays, lectures. 2. Decision-making—Case studies—Addresses, essays,
lectures. I. Park, Rolla Edward, ed. II. Christensen, Gary L., 1937- III. Western
Economic Association.
KF2844.A75R6   353.008'74'5547   73-6672
ISBN 0-669-88195-3

Published simultaneously in Canada.

Printed in the United States of America.

International Standard Book Number: 0-669-88195-3

Library of Congress Catalog Card Number: 73-6672

Contents

Preface

The papers in this collection make up a multi-viewpoint case study of the role played by analysis in the formulation of cable television regulatory policy. It is a contribution to the small but growing literature on the influence of analysis on decisions reached in complex political environments. Other recent works on this subject are by Alice M. Rivlin (1971), Clay Thomas Whitehead (1967), and Walter Williams (1971).

This collection is an outgrowth of a panel discussion at the annual meeting of the Western Economic Association in August 1972, where preliminary versions of the seven papers in Chapters 2 through 8 were presented. Revised versions of the papers, together with introductory and concluding chapters by the editor and an additional paper by Roger Noll (Chapter 9), constitute this volume.

The papers present the views of the authors as individuals. They should not be interpreted as the official opinion or policy of any of the organizations with which the authors are or have been associated.

This work was supported in part by The Rand Corporation using its own funds.

The Role of Analysis in
Regulatory Decisionmaking

1   Introduction

Rolla Edward Park

What are the relationships between policy analysis and policy decisions? This is an important question, not only because of the large cost of the efforts now being devoted to analysis, but even more so because of the very large potential benefit of effective analysis. We try to shed some light on the question here, hoping that more understanding of how analysis is *now* used will lead eventually to *improvements* in the way it is used.

We focus on one particular case: the adoption by the Federal Communications Commission early in 1972 of new regulations to govern cable television systems.

The new regulations came at the end of a decade of increasing FCC involvement with cable.[1] During that period, spokesmen for the affected industries—television broadcasters, cable television systems, the owners of copyrighted programs, television networks—argued forcefully for their various points of view. Many used research and analysis to support their positions. Other analyses were done by the FCC staff and by nonpartisan research organizations. All in all, this is a case in which the analytical inputs were unusually extensive and varied.

What effect did all of the analysis have on the regulations finally adopted? How was it used in the process that led up to adoption of the regulations? The papers in this collection present the views of eight people, all of whom participated in that process in one way or another.[2] The result is a multiple vantage point case study of the role of analysis in regulatory decisionmaking. I attempt to sketch a composite view in the concluding chapter.

Before we turn to the papers themselves, it may be useful to look in more detail at the questions we are trying to answer. The following list was prepared before the papers were written, to suggest to the contributors what subjects might be covered.

---

[1] Readers unfamiliar with the history of cable television and its regulation should read the appendixes to this volume. Appendix A is a brief history reprinted from the report of the Sloan Commission on Cable Communications (1971). Appendix B is a detailed chronology of federal regulation reprinted from Coll and Botein (1972).

[2] For brief biographies, see the "About the Contributors" section at the end of this collection

1. How did the views of the various participants on the likely impact of cable on broadcasting, and other issues, change over time? To what extent did changes in views result from (a) each participant's own analysis, (b) the analysis done by others and filed with the FCC? Are current views more confident than those held before the analyses? How did changes of view affect the policy outcome?

2. How is analysis evaluated? What are the roles of Commissioners, staff members, and competing analysts in evaluation? What aspects of analysis are most important in its evaluation: scholarly quality, clarity of presentation, outside publicity, congruence with preconceived ideas, etc.? Do the length, detail, and technical complexity of the analyses, coupled with limitations of staff and time, stand in the way of adequate evaluation?

3. Is there any essential difference between analysis by interested parties and analysis by others? Is the one any more likely to confirm prior views than is the other? Do they differ in their impact on the views of policymakers? On the views of interested parties?

4. What could have been done to make the analyses more useful than they were? Should the subjects treated, methods used, or style of presentation have been different? Would some modification of the adversary process result in more useful analysis?

This list does not serve as an exact outline for any of the papers, and not all of the questions are discussed by all of the contributors. But all of the questions are at least touched on someplace in the papers that follow.

2

A View from the President's Office of Telecommunications Policy[1]

Bruce M. Owen

Policy [science] is concerned with the contributions of systematic knowledge, structured rationality, and organized creativity to better policymaking. . . . [It] is essential for improvement of the human condition, and, indeed, for avoidance of catastrophe.

Yehezkel Dror (1971)

Policy analysis is supposed to bring rationality to government decisionmaking. Its role is to tell decisionmakers how to maximize output with given resources, or how to realize given objectives at least cost, or at least to quantify the costs and benefits of decisions made on arational grounds. This approach to policymaking has enjoyed a checkered career, and it has strong proponents and equally strong opponents.[2] The final line of defense for its proponents is that policymakers can hardly be worse off with additional information, provided the information itself is not very expensive. It is possible, however, that in some cases even this seemingly uncontroversial statement may be misleading.

First, let us steer clear of the thick underbrush of some normative issues. Policy decisions "ought" to be made by the constitutional process. Beyond that, I do not wish to go. The rest of this discussion will be about how (I think) policy *is* made, and why. It will also deal with the ways in which analysis can be useful to policymakers in making decisions *the way they do, or want to, make them.* It will be plain that as an economist I have serious misgivings about this process as it actually exists. But I have nothing much to add to the traditional literature by economists on how decisions ought to be made.

Cable television policy development during the past few years involved a number of different organizations within the Government.[3] The major players were the FCC, the Congress (several committees, especially those of Senators McClellan and Pastore, and Congressman MacDonald), the Office of Telecommunications Policy, and the Antitrust Division of the Department of Justice.

---

[1]At the time this paper was written, the author was Chief Economist of the Office of Telecommunications Policy, Executive Office of the President of the United States. Despite helpful comments and suggestions from Stanley Besen, Henry Goldberg, and Clay T. Whitehead, the views expressed here are the sole responsibility of the author.

[2]For discussion of policy sciences, see Dror (1971), Lindblom (1959), Lasswell (1971).

[3]For general discussions of the history of cable development and government reaction to it, see Johnson (1970a), Barnett (1970,1971) and Hochberg (1971).

The major private industry groups were represented by the National Association of Broadcasters,[4] the National Cable Television Association, and law firms representing the major copyright interests.[5] The three television networks represented themselves. Other trade groups did participate in the process, of course, as did other government agencies.

Each of the major industry representatives commissioned economic and legal studies and submitted these studies to the FCC and the other government agencies.[6] Economic and legal analysis was also carried out by several private groups not affiliated with a major vested interest. The most prominent of these were the Rand group and the Brookings-Yale group, but submissions were also made by a number of scholars and public interest groups, such as the ACLU.[7]

This paper is concerned with the development of cable television policy over the two years or so that ended with the FCC's rules published in February 1972. Still pending is an effort by the Executive Branch—the Cabinet committee on cable television policy—which will deal with long-term cable policy issues.[8] The discussion here is concerned mostly with the FCC's policy development, and some of the overall evaluation of the government's performance in this area may need to be modified when the Cabinet committee completes its work.

A Geologic Analogy

In order to understand the role of analysis in arriving at a final policy position, one must first understand the policy process itself. This can be compared to a kind of geological mechanism. Policy is determined by precedent, but pressures are continually building up on all sides of the status quo. Eventually, the pressures are sufficient to overcome inertia, and enough movement takes place to relieve the pressures. I do not want to imply that government always works this way, or that it should work this way, but merely that it does work this way in a large number of cases, and particularly in the case in question.

The pressures that make for change come from all sorts of places—political influence, economic interests, the press, technology, public opinion, public interest groups, and (sometimes) reform movements internal to the government itself. Inertia is supplied by tradition, but it is reinforced by pressures from groups that stand to lose from movements in policy away from the status quo. This whole process is by necessity political—after all, government decision-making can hardly fail to be political in the broadest sense—and many of the

---

[4] Along with the more adamantly anti-cable Association of Maximum Service Telecasters.

[5] Principally Nizer, Benjamin, Krim, and Ballon.

[6] See generally the references in the bibliography.

[7] It would be impractical even to list all those who filed comments in the FCC proceedings.

[8] See BROADCASTING (1972).

pressures are exerted in the traditional political ways. Every congressman and every appointed official feels such pressures on important issues. The regulatory agencies are no exception.[9]

Policy changes are almost always short-term or "muddling through" decisions, and are seen by the participants as such. The cable rules eventually arrived at, for instance, were regarded by the FCC as a temporary expedient to relieve the pressures that had been building up. Nothing was permanently "settled" as a conscious matter, although that may historically turn out to be the case. Policy in this model proceeds on a continuum. As in the geophysical analogy, the underlying "plate movements" are reality, to which the surface from time to time accommodates itself. Seldom does policy attempt to take the really long-term view that would arise from a thorough understanding of the underlying forces. It may be that this would not be good politics.

The preceding description of the policymaking process is, of course, an extreme oversimplification of a very complex structure. There are many instances of decisions that cannot be explained in these terms. Nevertheless, I believe this is a reasonable description (not an explanation) of the way things actually work a good deal of the time.

The FCC, in dealing with cable television, was faced with dynamic pressures from a number of sources. A good deal of the pressure was internal to the Commission. Other important early pressures came from the cable industry, the Justice Department, and public interest groups. The Antitrust Division saw cable as a competitive alternative to broadcasting, and championed it for that reason. By 1970, most FCC Commissioners apparently felt that movement was inevitable, at least on the bread and butter issue of distant signals. The inertial forces consisted of the broadcasting industry, the copyright owners, and their friends in Congress and the Executive Branch. There were, of course, also, inertial forces within the Commission and its staff. An event of major importance was the "legitimization" of cable through the creation of the CATV Task Force (later Cable Bureau) within the FCC. This gave the industry a promotional force within the Commission. At least equally important was the early commitment of the new FCC Chairman, Dean Burch, to get cable moving.[10]

It is not true that the officials in a position to make decisions were motivated solely by "political" pressures in the narrow sense of that term. Each official was influenced by the *substantive* arguments of one or more of the interest groups. But each one also had a vision of what was feasible or possible in a political

---

[9]It is sometimes difficult to understand the outrage of observers who decry decisions that are "politically motivated." How else is the political system supposed to function? References must be to underlying inequities in the political system itself; it is both unrealistic and unfair to expect officials to always "rise above it."

[10]For general descriptions of these forces, there is no better source than contemporary issues of BROADCASTING magazine.

sense, and of the consequences to the public and themselves of making a serious mistake. This vision of feasibility and consequences tends to be a conservative influence, and the inertial interest groups play up the very real adverse risks of mistakes.

It is here that analysis can be very important. Economic and technical analysis attempts to provide predictions of the consequences of movements in policies. If the information thus supplied is viewed as accurate and convincing, the risk of movement is reduced, and policy change becomes more likely. Analysis can be equally important in showing the interest groups which side their bread is buttered on. Taken at face value, the polemics of some of the anti-cable groups would seem to indicate ignorance of some of the long-term benefits of cable to themselves. Obviously, those effects most amenable to quantification are the easiest to deal with in this context. It is not surprising, then, that most of the economic analysis supplied to the FCC dealt with the consequences of relaxing the ban on distant signals, and with the consequences of varying degrees of copyright liability therefor. Relatively little analysis dealt with such questions as licensing of cable systems, content regulation, or alternative structures for the cable industry of the future.[11]

The value of economic analysis commissioned by the economic interest groups is limited by the identity of its sponsors, no matter how impressive the credentials of the researchers. Thus, the economic analysis submitted by the industry groups could essentially be predicted in advance, and (while of potential use in rationalizing the final decision) could not be expected to make much difference to the attitudes of the officials. This tendency is, of course, aggravated by the absence of high-quality, in-house FCC capability to evaluate the research results submitted by the adversaries. It is not that the FCC and other agencies do not have good people on their staffs. They do. But they do not have enough of them to do an adequate job of evaluating sophisticated analysis. Also, particularly in this instance, the staffs were themselves polarized to some extent on the policy issues involved.

Finally, it appears unfortunately to be the case that most of the issues involved—and particularly the question of distant signal impact on station viability—were sufficiently difficult that analysts disagreed on the effects that would result from given policies. This situation was not improved by the use of a wide variety of initial assumptions among the various analyses. In the end, the Commission dismissed the impact analysis almost entirely on the ground that the experts disagreed. It made no serious attempt to determine who was right.[12]

---

[11]Important exceptions do exist. See Johnson (1970a), Task Force (1968a, 1968b), Barnett (1970,1972), Smith (1970), Jones (1970), among others.

[12]See FCC (1972a) at paragraphs 69 and 70. One problem is that commissioners are usually lawyers who, while they can and will resolve legal arguments proposed by contending parties, are not prepared to resolve technical economic questions. One solution is to raise the economic expertise of the commission and its staff.

The Dynamic and Inertial Forces

The broadcasting industry felt that any expansion of cable television was bound in the end to be partly at its expense. This is probably true considering most of the probable future paths of the industry.[13] The question of distant signals, regarded as crucial by the cable industry, was therefore an issue for broadcasters, regardless of the effect this particular phenomenon, in itself, might be expected to have on them.[14] It would have made no real difference if an increase in imported distant signals could be proved to increase all braodcasters' profits, if in the end cable grew into a serious threat to broadcasters on other fronts. Futurists, talking glibly about cable "replacing" over-the-air broadcasting, scared the industry to death.

The cable industry regarded distant signals as essential to its further growth. Several analysts suggested that this was not a necessary or even a sufficient condition for serious penetration of the top 100 markets. Perhaps this issue was also, in part, a symbolic one for the cable industry. Perhaps distant signals were thought to be sufficient to begin the process of entrenchment that is traditionally followed by regulatory nurturing.

The copyright owners were often forced into ambiguous positions. On the one hand, importation of distant signals, with or without pooled copyright payments, threatened to disrupt profitable exclusivity arrangements and thus reduce present revenues. On the other hand, the copyright owners saw the growth of cable as a long-term gain for their industry, particularly in the realm of pay-TV. On several occasions, the copyright owners found themselves between the broadcast and cable interests, trying to bring about a compromise settlement of the distant signal issue.[15]

Policymakers entering this arena were faced not only with the economic conflicts, but with certain substantive public interest considerations. Clearly,

---

[13] At best broadcasters will be faced with increasing competition that reduces the value of a broadcast license and thus threatens the loss of scarcity rent capitalized at the time the license was purchased.

[14] Analysis of the impact of distant signals *per se* was therefore slightly beside the point so far as broadcast opposition to cable was concerned.

[15] Copyright owners derive most of their television revenue from the top 50 or 60 markets. This partially explains the structure of the FCC's final distant signal rules. The Committee of Copyright Owners represented the major Hollywood studios. A substantial part of the syndication market is, however, controlled by the networks, or at least was until the "prime time access" rules went into effect. The networks were therefore interested in the cable question not only as broadcasters but also as copyright owners. Copyright legislation in Congress had been held up pending the FCC's resolution of the cable issues, but the FCC kept tossing the ball back to the Congress. The district court decision in the CBS VS. TELEPROMPTER suit has since further clouded the copyright issue. Previous agreements had been reached between the cable and broadcasting interests (spring 1969) and between the copyright and cable interests (summer 1971), but both broke down.

cable had many potential public benefits. Clearly, widespread bankruptcy of broadcast stations would deprive the public of benefits that cable could not, in the immediate future, replace.[16] Clearly, it was "unfair" to copyright owners to have their material used without reward.

The television networks also played a role in this process. Like the copyright owners, they were in a position perhaps to gain in the long-term from cable growth, but they seemed to believe that they would suffer short-term losses from distant signal importation. The economic and political power of the networks put them in a position to push for a settlement somewhat more in their favor than might otherwise be the case.

The behavior of the networks remains something of a mystery. It is not clear that they acted in their own long-term interest in their partially successful attempt to stall cable growth. They were perhaps motivated in part by their relationship with affiliates.[17] Whatever the motivation (and all three networks were not equally concerned), their influence, combined with the political influence of local broadcasters (as perceived by officials), was very important in determining the final outcome.

Relief of Pressure

All of these pressures culminated in the August 5, 1971 "letter of intent" from the FCC to Congress.[18] The letter of intent laid out an interim solution to the distant signal problem and, in addition, some longer-term structural and regulatory proposals. The distant signal proposals were responsive to the pressures of the competing interest groups, rather than to any formal analysis of costs and benefits to the public. These costs and benefits did influence the decision, but only on an impressionistic basis. The number of distant signals that could be imported was set as high as the Commission thought it could go without forcing an overwhelming response from the broadcast industry in the form of Congressional and Executive Branch pressure. Of course, this was not regarded as a once-and-for-all movement, but merely an interim expedient for relief of pressure along a continuum.

The August 5 proposals did not, however, deal with the exclusivity question, regarded as essential by the copyright interests. Any resolution of this issue would work in favor of the broadcasters. The number of distant signals allowed on August 5 was also seen by broadcasters as "only the beginning." The absence of any resolution of the patently unfair copyright-exclusivity issue, combined

---

[16] Quite aside from the economic threat to public service programming; see below.

[17] Note also their interests as copyright holders in the syndication market.

[18] FCC (1971b).

with the potential threat of broadcast industry-inspired Congressional activity, led the groups to engage in further negotiations.[19]

Negotiations continued throughout the fall of 1971, with the OTP and FCC trying to work out a compromise agreement acceptable to the parties. These efforts did result in an agreement announced on November 11, 1971.[20] The compromise or "consensus" agreement was an extremely complicated document, and in part an ambiguous one. This result was perhaps inevitable, given the complexity of the issues and the nature of compromises. But the complexity itself may have been responsible for the success of the negotiations. At the time the compromise was reached, none of the parties, and certainly not the Government, had the slightest idea of its detailed consequences. There was no quantitative analysis of the probable effects of the complex exclusivity arrangements. Decisionmakers and the parties did, of course, have some idea of the bounds of those effects.

The absence of analytic information on the effects of the compromise may have been largely responsible for the agreement. Each side probably felt that it would be helped—the broadcasters by the mere existence of exclusivity protection, the cable operators by the provision allowing unrestricted importation to fill "holes" left by blacked-out programs. But no one knew how many "holes" there would be, or what the costs of filling them with other imported material might amount to.[21]

Thus, the absence of policy analysis may have facilitated an agreement viewed by officials as an end in itself. The conduct of analysis by the government itself would not have been of any particular use, even if kept secret, since the object was to give the cable interests as much interim growth incentive through distant signals as was consistent with broadcast acquiescence. No one believed that distant signals were the key to long-term cable growth, but any rules that lay between the status quo and the August 5 proposals were presumed (reasonably) to give "something" to the cable interests, whose growth was seen as being in the public interest.

Some Deeper Dynamic Forces

Why was cable growth seen as being in the public interest? Here, independent analysis was important. The work at Rand and elsewhere was quite convincing in

---

[19]The context in which these further negotiations took place would be an interesting political study in itself. The broad outlines can be followed in contemporary issues of BROADCASTING.

[20]BROADCASTING (1971b), and Barnett (1972), fn. 26.

[21]This question has since been analyzed by Park (1972c).

its demonstration of cable's potential benefits, and in alleviating the fears of officials that the broadcast industry would in fact be seriously hurt. Throughout the 1960s, there had been a great outpouring of academic and intellectual interest in cable. It probably began with Barnett and Greenberg and reached a highpoint with Ralph Lee Smith.[22] This created a climate of opinion that was crucial to cable's prospects. The "analysis" was motivated not only by disinterested policy research, but also by intellectual dissatisfaction with existing television performance. The intellectuals, as a group, were not "unbiased." They were clearly favorable to cable, aside from its substantive merits. This was important in overcoming what can only be described as the somewhat "scruffy" and unprofessional demeanor of the cable industry. Unused to Washington, they tended to present an unfavorable contrast to the smoother and more experienced broadcast representatives in dealing with Federal officials.[23] Such factors were not unimportant, and the intellectuals made cable more respectable. Thus, the *direction* in which policy should move was influenced by policy analysis, or at least by intellectual opinion, while the length or *extent* of movement in that direction was circumscribed by what (for want of a better expression) I shall describe as political considerations. And what was important to the latter problem was the extent to which broadcasters *thought*, or convinced others they thought, they would be hurt. No responsible public official was about to take any serious risk of seeming to deprive the public of "free" over-the-air television.

Aside from the cataclysmic threat of the actual demise of broadcast stations, there was a problem of the quality of broadcast service. That is, the profits of broadcasters are used by the FCC to subsidize public service programming.[24] Threats to the profitability of broadcast stations thus have public interest connotations. Although never addressed explicitly, there is a sense in which the Commission is concerned with maintaining a "reasonable" rate of return in the broadcast industry in order to support these merit goods. This doctrine has received judicial approval.[25]

In all the fuss about distant signals, some very important questions got neglected.[26] These were principally such issues as industry structure, regulation, licensing, and ownership. Being of less immediate political consequence, these issues were more susceptible to influence by careful policy analysis. Yet, we ended up with such policy freaks as the so-called "N+1" rule and "certificates of compliance" and reserved free channels for special purposes. How did this happen?

---

[22]Barnett and Greenberg (1968); Smith (1972). For papers that appeared between these points in time, see the bibliography.

[23]The cable industry was neither more nor less self-interested than the other parties. They were less experienced in dealing with the policy process and perhaps less willing to recognize the necessity for compromise.

[24]See Posner (1971).

[25]Carroll Broadcasting v. FCC, 258 F. 2d, 440 (D.C. Cir., 1958).

[26]Here, it should be emphasized, the discussion concerns the FCC rules. The story has not ended, since the Cabinet committee has yet to report on its study of long-term policy.

The deficiencies in the long-term aspects of the cable rules can be traced to a number of causes. They were partly the result of a compromise within the Commission between proponents of a populist, pro-cable position and more "realistic" opinion. They were partly traceable, too, to their lack of immediacy in the political context—a deferrable set of issues. Even the independent policy analysts got caught up in the distant signal question, and talked about the broader structural and regulatory issues only in rather abstract and theoretical terms. As a result, these portions of the rules were largely created by staffs accustomed to thinking in terms of the traditional broadcast and common carrier arrangements, and not sufficiently attuned to the unique opportunities and dangers of the new medium. Also, there was considerable ambiguity about the authority of the FCC to make rules on these matters before the Supreme Court had made its Midwest Video decision.[27] Finally, long-term rules were seen as "soft" decisions, easily changed later or waived in particular cases, and thus not a matter for serious concern. Indeed, in the early drafts of the new rules, waivers were the first subject treated.

Anticipating some of these problems, the President established a Cabinet-level committee in June 1971 to study cable and to provide him with options for long-term policy. This committee also played an indirect role in the resolution of the short-term issues. It was originally scheduled to report in the fall of 1971, but the compromise agreement relieved the pressure on that deadline, and the growing awareness that legislation would be required to deal with the long-term issues led the committee to extend its deliberations.

Policy analysis dealing with alternative industry structures and long-term regulatory policies turned out to be very scarce. Aside from some distinguished work by Leland Johnson and some staff papers prepared for the Sloan Commission, there wasn't much to go on.[28] Accordingly, most of the supporting analysis for the committee was done in-house by the OTP staff, with help from other government agencies.[29] The various industry groups turned out to have relatively little to add to their FCC submissions, but these submissions were largely addressed to different issues. Industry was not accustomed to the government trying consciously to create long-term policy.

The committee and its staff would have been greatly aided by extensive and imaginative analysis of long-term policy questions, as would the FCC and eventually the Congress. This is one case in which the contributions of independent analysis were, on the whole, not sufficiently theoretical and imaginative—surely an anomalous instance.

---

[27]Midwest Video was settled in favor of the FCC in May 1972.

[28]Kestenbaum (1971), Pemberton (1971), Jones (1970), Johnson (1970a).

[29]The report of this committee may have been released by the time this paper is published. Since the author participated in its development, no other comments on it would be appropriate here.

The Role of Analysis

The major contributions of analysis to the resolution of cable policy took two forms. First, analysis (in the broadest sense) in the years preceding 1971 helped to build up a climate of opinion conducive to a relaxation of the freeze on cable growth. Academic and other independent analysts, nearly unanimous in their support of the virtues of cable technology, constituted an important decentralized pressure group for change. They made cable respectable.[30] This pressure gradually percolated up to the policymakers and affected their basic attitudes toward cable. Second, analysis was important in the formation of policy itself, partly by reducing the concern of public officials that cable would seriously hurt broadcasters in the short run, and partly by emphasizing the costs of the various proposals of claimants on the "surplus."[31]

The absence of analysis was important, on the other hand, in making a compromise agreement possible on the distant signal issue.

If there was any broad failure of analysis, it was in two areas. First, there was insufficient attention to long-term structural and regulatory issues. Second, there was very little (public) analysis directed to the affected industries, and particularly little addressed to the question of how broadcasters might stand to gain from cable growth. If, as seems reasonable, everyone including the broadcasters regarded *some* relaxation of the cable freeze as inevitable, then the broadcasters ought to have been provided with more clues to where their ultimate advantage lay. Some possibilities in the ownership and channel leasing area are obvious.[32]

What does this experience teach us about policy analysis in general? The case is perhaps a bad one, since there was more than an average amount of narrowly political constraint involved in the cable issues.[33] But some things are clear. First, independent academic or non-profit policy research activity is much more influential than industry-sponsored research. Industry-sponsored analysis does not supply policymakers with additional analytic information because its results are predictable.[34] But there was relatively little independent and academic research on the cable question in comparison with the work done by the interest

---

[30]Perhaps the virtue of "respectability" in the eyes of regulators should be added to the traditional list of barriers to entry.

[31]That is, profits of the cable industry in excess of those necessary to attract entry. See McGowan, Noll, and Peck (1971b).

[32]The FCC had barred broadcasters from same-market ownership of cable systems. There exist some regulatory structures for cable, such as common carrier status, in which this is not really necessary. Anyway, the effect was the same as barring buggy whip manufacturers from owning gasoline stations. They had no alternative but to fight for delay of the inevitable.

[33]It is axiomatic that an issue involving the economic interests of the major mass media will be politicized.

[34]Industry analysis does provide data, and it does of course constitute part of the partisan ARGUMENT, and may be convincing in that light.

groups. There ought to be some better mechanism for the production of independent research. (OTP and NSF are trying to work out some specific projects in this area.) Second, there could usefully have been a lot more emphasis in the policy analysis on the longer-term issues, and still can be. It is precisely on these issues that the independent researcher is likely to be most influential if he can do the right kind of analysis, since the political influences are less strong. Third, independent policy analysis can be very useful in creating a climate of opinion conducive to change, but only with significant lags. Policy analysis submitted late in the game is likely to be ignored unless it is actually lobbied—personally forced on officials who do not read routine filings or the current academic literature. This lobbying effort can be very expensive, but it is the only effective substitute for a long lead time. Independent and academic research can seldom be done in response to specific needs from Washington that have any urgency. By the time a policymaker recognizes the need for research, it is too late to commission anything but staff or consulting activity. Clearly, then, more independent policy analysis is going to have to be carried out in anticipation of policymakers' needs.

Conclusion

When all is said and done, policy decisions are made not by the experts but by public officials. The experts advise the decisionmaker, but they provide only one of many components in the decisionmaking process. A very great deal of the content of policy can be traced to tradition and to prejudice—or to what one of my colleagues calls "religion." These influences are really no different in kind than the initial assumptions that precede the most sophisticated analysis. One should not canonize "gut-reaction" policymakers, but neither should one put excessive emphasis on analytic tools that indicate contrary directions—tools that often are based on assumptions and ideas antithetical to those of public officials. Cable television policy was and is being developed (both at the FCC and elsewhere) largely without the aid of analysis in any strict sense. This can be traced, at least in part, to the unwillingness of analysts to understand and accept the initial assumptions and objective functions of politicians. No doubt the latter are often wrong from some abstract public interest standpoint, and it is perhaps then not altogether lamentable that their decisions are not cloaked in the garb of "policy science."

An economist in Washington spends a lot of time trying to persuade non-economists to accept his prejudices. These are resisted both because they sometimes imply threats to traditional practices in which officials have a vested interest, and because they often imply values alien to others. When this happens, one is inevitably thrown back to arguments about assumptions, not analytic logic. It has been my experience that the economist's assumptions are often no easier to defend than those of others. What does one do with a public official who simply does not *want* to maximize, minimize, or optimize anything? Such attitudes need not be irrational. In such a forum, the economist or analyst can either accept the role of "go-for" or he can enter the debate as one of many contending interests, none of whom has any monopoly on truth.

3

A View from the National Cable Television Association[1]

Gary L. Christensen

My thesis is that economic research and analysis plays little part in the regulator's decisionmaking, but does play a substantial role in the decision-making of those who are regulated, even though that role is not a controlling one. How does one conclude that economic analyses played little or no part in effecting regulatory decisionmaking? The answer is to turn to the regulator's language itself.

In 1963, the Commission made its first move to regulate a cable television system.[2] It proposed applying the same strictures to all microwave-served cable television systems in a rulemaking proceeding that led to the *First Report and Order on CATV* (1965). In that proceeding three economic studies were filed: the Fisher Report (1964), sponsored by the National Association of Broadcasters; the Arkin Report (1964), sponsored by the National Cable Television Association; and the Seiden Report (1965), commissioned by the Federal Communications Commission. In the *First Report and Order*, the FCC concluded:

By far the most ambitious effort to demonstrate the effect of CATV competition upon the audience and revenues of television broadcasters, however, is contained in the Fisher Report, appended to the NAB's reply comments. . . .

The bulk of the Fisher Report (pp. 5-96) is devoted to a detailed explanation of the statistical procedures followed in the analyses, the factors or variables considered, the manner in which they were treated and why, the quantitative results obtained and the basis for each subsidiary conclusion drawn. . . .

The Report concluded that there is a direct correlation between increases in audience size and station revenues.

. . . The Fisher Report further concluded (pp. 31-37) that small stations, which are on the average less profitable than large stations, have operating expenses which are more sensitive to changes in revenue than those of large market stations and that when a small market station's revenue falls, it can be expected to cut expenditures relatively more than will a large market station. . . . Using a variety of measures, Dr. Fisher shows that if his basic projections are correct, the impact of CATV non-carriage, duplication or simple fractionalization of station audience through additional program choices upon the profits of

---

[1] The author was formerly General Counsel with the National Cable Television Association. He is now a member of Hogan and Hartson, Attorneys at Law, Washington, D.C. The opinions expressed here are his alone.

[2] Carter Mountain Transmission Corporation (1963).

15

a large number of stations can be serious and, in the case of stations already marginal, disastrous.

These conclusions corresponded with the FCC's previous *Carter Mountain* decision. The FCC also found:

In order to evaluate the Fisher Report, NCTA retained Dr. Herbert Arkin. . . . In Dr. Arkin's opinion, 'the conclusions in the report, about the effect of CATV subscriptions on the financial position of local television stations, are at best of dubious validity and at worst a possible complete misstatement.' He bases this opinion on a set of criticisms of the report's logic, its statistical techniques and the data which it utilizes.

The comments of the parties center upon the effect which CATV competition has, or may be expected to have, upon television broadcast service. We must evaluate this effect, however, in light of our statutory responsibilities. We must also take into account the basic conditions under which CATV systems and television broadcasting stations compete as alternative means for the distribution of television programs. . . .

The goal is thus a commercial television system which will (1) be truly competitive on a national scale by making provision for at least four commercial stations in all large centers of population; (2) provide at least three competitive facilities in all medium-sized communities; and (3) permit all communities of appreciable size to have at least one television station as an outlet for local self-expression.

These considerations, all expressed or inherent in our *Carter Mountain* decision, lead to certain broad conclusions:

(1) If there is a significant risk that CATV competition will destroy or seriously degrade the service offered by a television broadcaster, our statutory duties require us to seek means to prevent this result. . . .

(2) It is therefore inappropriate to equate competition between broadcasting stations with competition between broadcasting and CATV. . . .

(3) We cannot properly ignore this problem until and unless it is raised in the context of individual adjudicative cases. . . .

(4) This is not in any way to ignore or to denigrate the very real contribution which CATV service makes to the public interest. Our conclusion is rather that community antenna television serves the public interest when it acts as a supplement rather than a substitute for off-the-air television service. The question at the heart of these proceedings is whether and to what extent rule making action is necessary or appropriate to integrate CATV service into our existing television system—to ensure that CATV performs its valuable supplementary role without unduly damaging or impeding the growth of television broadcast service. . . .

Now, as in 1959, we think it impossible, with the data at hand, to isolate reliably the effects of CATV competition from all of the other factors which operate to produce particular financial results in differing settings. The Fisher Report, in our view, marks a substantial advance toward the goal of isolating and predicting the effects of CATV competition, and we think many of the criticisms leveled at that report by other parties are misplaced. But there remain a number of questions. The Fisher Report assumes that a small decline in reported station circulation is followed by an equivalent decline in the prices advertisers are willing to pay. The Report furnishes no specific evidence of this fact, and our experience is that—particularly where national advertisers deal with smaller markets—there is much less tendency to react to small changes in station audience. There is also a question concerning the extent to which the various conditions described in Dr. Fisher's conclusions (as to non-carriage and duplication where the subscriber was previously able to receive one or more stations) are present in practice. *Without further exploration of these and other questions, we would not and do not rely upon Dr. Fisher's conclusions as to the dollar effects of CATV competition and their significance in different settings.*

To suggest that the likelihood of serious impact can therefore be dismissed, however, is to misconceive entirely the terms on which the problem comes to us. Now, as in 1959, it is plain that CATV competition can have a substantial negative effect upon station audience and revenues, although we lack the tools with which to measure precisely the degree of such impact.

Prediction of particular results in particular cases must, of course, remain hazardous. As a general matter, it remains true that there is no way to predict with reliability the results of individual cases.[3]

So, the FCC imposed general rules consistent with its previous action, which had been taken *prior* to the submission of professional economic analyses. The FCC also announced its intention to expand those rules to all cable television systems, by a rulemaking proceeding that led to the *Second Report and Order.* In the *Second Report and Order*, the FCC found:

In view of the rapidly changing circumstances outlined above, we can see no point in conducting a further fact-finding inquiry with respect to non-microwave CATV as it has existed in the past. The extensive studies conducted by Dr. Fisher, Dr. Seiden and NCTA in conjunction with Docket Nos. 14895 and 15233, and further studies of CBS and AMST in this proceeding, all concerned non-microwave as well as microwave CATV systems. *Studies of this nature are out-of-date almost before we have had time to consider them. Moreover, they are of limited value since they cannot measure some of the most important factors we are bound to consider.* These include the cumulative future effect of greater penetration by CATV systems franchised or applied for but not yet in operation, the degree of success to be achieved by CATV systems in big cities or other well-served areas, and the effect of the burgeoning CATV activity—if left unregulated—on the decisions of potential applicants and existing licensees as to whether to inaugurate or improve service. . . .

In sum, we have concluded in the First Report and Order in Docket Nos. 14895 and 15233 that the public interest requires that CATV systems carry local stations without duplication for a reasonable period, in order to avoid unfair competitive disadvantage to and prejudicial effect on existing and potential broadcast service. We have concluded herein that we have authority under the present provisions of the Communications Act to extend these requirements to non-microwave systems. In view of the rapid surge in CATV growth since this proceeding was initiated, we think that our statutory obligations require us to act now in the areas we have proposed. This will end the present unwarranted distinction between microwave and non-microwave systems, and will enable us to make the rules effective before operations are

---

[3]FCC (1965). Emphasis added.

commenced by a large number of CATV proposals presently in the franchise or application stage.[4]

So much for the ambitious efforts at economic analysis aiding policymakers in the early regulatory stages. But, after eight years of regulating cable television, with reams of papers having been submitted, hearings having been conducted, and valuable, sophisticated economic reports having been filed with the FCC, we could expect more. Yet, in the latest *Cable Television Report*, the FCC found:

The conflicting conclusions of these studies make abundantly clear the difficulties involved in attempting to predict the future where there are so many variables and unknowns. *While the reports and studies have been useful in illuminating the various elements of our policy decision, we cannot rely on any particular report or study as a sure barometer of the future. We would simply point out there is no consensus, and we do not pretend that we can now forecast precisely how cable will evolve in major markets. There is inherent uncertainty.* But this does not mean that we should stand still and block all possibility of new and diverse communications benefits. Rather, it means that we should act in a conservative, pragmatic fashion—in the sense of maintaining the present system and adding to it in a significant way, taking a sound and realistic first step and then evaluating our experience. That is the approach we have taken.[5]

So, the Commission enacted into regulatory language a compromise which was agreed upon only under strong political coercion.

While I can speak only from my experience in the cable television industry, the studies submitted to the FCC, as well as those privately available, were weighed very carefully by the leaders in the cable television industry before positions were taken or agreements entered into. Each of the issues raised by economic analysts were considered and given priorities for the near-term future. I believe that less weight was given to those issues and conclusions for the long-term future because it was felt that underlying data, assumptions, and the policy environment would change.

In the end, I leave you to draw your own conclusions.

---

[4] FCC (1966). Emphasis added.

[5] FCC (1972a). Emphasis added.

4

A View from the National Association of Broadcasters[1]

John A. Dimling, Jr.

"Let us sit on this log at the roadside," says I, "and forget the inhumanity and ribaldry of the poets. It is in the glorious columns of ascertained facts and legalized measures that beauty is to be found. In this very log we sit upon, Mrs. Sampson," says I, "is statistics more wonderful than any poem. The rings show it was 60 years old. At the depth of 2000 feet it would become coal in 3000 years. The deepest coal mine in the world is at Killingworth, near Newcastle. A box four feet long, three feet wide, and two feet eight inches deep will hold one ton of coal. If an artery is cut, compress it above the wound. A man's leg contains thirty bones. The Tower of London was burned in 1841."

"Go on, Mr. Pratt," says Mrs. Sampson. "Them ideas is so original and soothing. I think statistics are just as lovely as they can be."

O. Henry, *The Handbook of Hymen*
as quoted in Kendall and Stuart (1961)

The principal focus of the discussion in this paper is on the role of analysis in the formulation of one specific aspect of cable policy—the importation of distant signals by cable systems, the subject of FCC Docket 18397-A. This is the area in which I've been most involved, and in which the National Association of Broadcasters has done research. Beyond that, the distant signal question has been a central one for cable policy for the last ten years. Finally, compared to many areas of communications policy, the distant signal question is relatively susceptible to research.

Before turning to Docket 18397-A, however, I might offer the observation that, at least in a general way, research and analysis have indeed played a role in the formulation of cable policy. Peter Steiner (1952) could perhaps be considered the intellectual godfather of much of what has been written about cable; certainly his pointing out that program diversity increases with the number of broadcast channels whetted the interest in cable of writers and policymakers concerned with achieving greater diversity in television programming. Also, I might reiterate the observation of Barnett and Greenberg that cable, like negotiable certificates of deposit and containerized rail transportation, has seemed to hold a special place in the hearts of those who believe in free

---

[1]The views expressed in this paper are the author's and not necessarily those of the National Association of Broadcasters.

19

markets.[2] In short, the net effect of the work of a number of economists, political scientists, and legal researchers has been to create an environment in which cable is regarded as having potential for curing some, if not all, of the nation's ills.

Analysis in Docket 18397-A

Perhaps the best way to discuss the impact of research in this area is first to make some assessment of what the research shows, and then to comment on how the policy reflected, or failed to reflect, the research results. This approach will be used in discussing two questions that seem to have been central in Docket 18397-A:

1. Does the development of cable in the top 100 markets require that cable systems import distant signals?
2. What would be the impact of distant signals on local television stations?

The Necessity for Distant Signals

As has been noted above, implicit in cable policy has been the assumption that expansion and development of cable is desirable. From the FCC's point of view, this assumption led naturally to the question, "What must be done to get the cable laid?" Because the cable industry had taken the position that carriage of distant signals was necessary for success in the larger television markets, the Commission in Docket 18397 invited the cable industry "to engage in a test to determine the efficacy of CATV operation in a major market, providing excellent reception of local signals (particularly useful as to color and in some homes UHF), automatic services (e.g., news, time, weather, stock ticker), and programming procured by the cable by entering the competitive TV program-ming market (either by outright origination or by re-transmission consent)"[3]—in other words, to find out if distant signals were necessary. In Docket 18397-A, the Commission noted that the cable industry had been uninterested in such a test; in spite of this lack of interest (or perhaps because of it) the Commission then put forward the commercial substitution scheme to allow cable systems to import distant signals.

Given the central importance of this issue, and the Commission's obvious interest in obtaining data about the importance of distant signals, it seemed reasonable to expect that considerable research attention would be devoted to

---

[2] Barnett and Greenberg (1969).
[3] FCC (1970b), paragraph 3.

the question, and that the Commission would carefully evaluate whatever material was submitted. This did not happen. Relatively little material was submitted, and, surprisingly, the material that was submitted (some by other contributors to this volume) did *not* demonstrate that the success of cable system depends on importing distant signals.

As part of their elaborate analysis of the impact of regulation on the cable industry, Professors Comanor and Mitchell used regression analysis to develop equations to estimate the demand for cable. These equations predict the effect of various factors, including the number of distant signals carried by a cable system, on the fraction of potential customers that will become cable subscribers. Their results indicate that the availability of distant signals does not have a statistically significant effect on cable penetration. In the six equations of Tables 2 and 4 in their report,[4] the largest t-value for the coefficients on the "independent stations" variable is 0.90, and in general, the t-values are lower for the "independent stations" coefficients than for other variables in their analyses.

The comments filed in Docket 18397-A by McGowan, Noll, and Peck contained similar results concerning the effect of distant signals on the demand for cable service. As they point out, their Table 4 indicates that the coefficient describing the effect of additional independent signals on cable penetration is not significantly different from zero by conventional statistical standards. I find their discussion of this coefficient somewhat confusing, however, and it occurs to me that a reader with no statistical background might be (or might have been) unintentionally misled by several of the statements made by the authors. They say, for example, "Thus, the best that can be said on the basis of the present results is that the response of CATV subscribership to increases in the number of independent station alternatives offered is highly likely to be in the range of 0 to 0.15."[5] By selecting 0.15 as an upper bound, they may give the impression that such a bound is suggested by a conventional interpretation of their results, rather than selected because the "duplicate network" coefficient is 0.15.[6]

Finally, Park's study filed after the deadline for comments in Docket 18397-A, is probably the most comprehensive analysis of factors that affect cable penetration. Park's equations explain substantially more of the variation in the dependent penetration variable than do other analyses (r^2 is .73 for his Equation (1), Table 2; and .75 for his Equation (*)).[7] Even with these more powerful equations, Park concludes—on the basis of his analysis of the additional

---

[4]Comanor and Mitchell (1970), pp. 11, 16.

[5]McGowan, Noll, and Peck (1971a), p. 16.

[6]Perhaps a more direct reason for according little weight to the lack of statistical significance of the "independent variable" coefficient is that the model itself seems somewhat suspect, since the negative coefficient on income and the positive coefficient on price seem somewhat unreasonable—is cable really a Giffin type of good? See McGowan, Noll, and Peck (1971b), for their more sophisticated model.

[7]Park (1971c), p. 22.

variance explained by each independent variable (Table 3)—that the coefficient for the independent station variable is not significant at the .05 level.

(Actually, in Park's analysis using a revised maturity factor,[8]—Line (*) in his Table 2—it appears that the independent stations coefficient may be significant at the .05 level on a one-tailed test, but he does not repeat the analysis of variance using Equation (*).)

One interpretation of these results is that cable penetration is not sensitive to distant signal carriage, and that distant signals are not, therefore, necessary for the success of cable. I would like to suggest a more conservative interpretation: that the studies filed in Docket 18397-A give little evidence that distant signals have much impact on penetration. To put it more precisely, if one were to test the hypothesis that distant signals do not affect penetration, then (on the basis of the results discussed here) that hypothesis could not be rejected.

Impact on Television Stations

A great deal of the research filed in Docket 18397-A dealt with the impact on local stations of cable importation of distant signals. Indeed, in a somewhat unusual and certainly commendable step, the Commission itself directed the Broadcast Bureau's research chief to provide research material on the interface between cable and over-the-air television, and then released the study for comments. Taken as a whole, there were areas of substantial agreement between the research submitted by various organizations and individuals, and there were, of course, areas of disagreement.

Taking the easy part first (the areas of agreement), I might begin by observing that it seems unfortunate that the extent of agreement in much of the research on distant signal impact was ignored or perhaps not recognized by many observers and participants in Docket 18397-A. One of the leading trade papers, for instance, headlined its coverage of the docket, "Coming Up—Battle of CATV Statisticians." Certainly various attorneys indicated privately that the filings corroborated their feeling that "researchers will prove anything you want them to prove." I think, therefore, that it is worth noting the extent to which a consistent picture emerged from the research.

The first area of agreement was the extent to which local stations would lose audience to imported independents. An analysis filed by NAB, for example, suggested that in a three-station market, average audience loss by local stations to four imported independent stations would average about 19 percent if half the households in the market were cable subscribers. Using a more sophisticated analysis, Park (1970) estimated that the audience loss in prime time would average about 18 percent over all television markets, and material submitted by other broadcasters indicated similar audience losses.

[8]Park (1971c), p. 26.

To the extent that the research studies considered the relation between station audience and station revenue, they also agreed that a very direct relation exists between the two quantities. Earlier research had demonstrated a strong linear relation between revenue and audience;[9] Park also found this, but discovered that a curvilinear function described the relation even better. A different sort of refinement was suggested both by NAB (1970) and M.H. Seiden and Associates (1970) and acknowledged by Park. Because advertising revenue generated by network programs is split between networks and stations, the value of a station's audience varies by day part—station revenue per viewing household is greater in early fringe time, for example, than it is in prime time. Thus, while the relation between audience and revenue within a day part may be a nearly linear one, the slope is different for different day parts. Using data from Broadcast Advertiser Reports, the NAB filing estimated that 24 percent of station revenues were earned in the 5-7:30 PM day part, and 32 percent were earned during prime time (7:30-11 PM). Seiden surveyed 21 stations to estimate revenue by day part; a special tabulation of his data, with an estimate of network revenue added to the non-network revenue reported by survey respondents, estimated that early fringe accounted for 24 percent of station revenues, and prime time for 33 percent. Because stations are likely to lose relatively larger fractions of their audiences to imported stations in early fringe time than in prime time, the higher revenue per household in early fringe time indicates that overall revenue loss would be somewhat greater than the average audience loss.

Impact on UHF Stations

Several areas of significant disagreement emerged in Docket 18397-A. The most interesting of these, from an analytic viewpoint, is the effect of cable on UHF stations. On the negative side, UHF stations would be subject to audience fractionalization in the same way as VHF stations; potentially counterbalancing this is the ability of cable to eliminate the UHF "handicap." As broken down by Park (1970, 1971a), this handicap consists of tuning difficulties, reception problems (due either to antenna or transmission difficulties), and limited UHF set penetration. Since normal replacement of television sets will lead to virtually complete UHF penetration within just a few years, assessment of cable's ability to overcome the UHF handicap should concentrate on tuning and reception difficulties. A number of different estimates of the UHF handicap were filed in Docket 18397-A, and I will not attempt to evaluate or even describe them here. I would like to discuss what seems to me to have been a fundamental error in much of the analysis submitted—the failure to assess the effect of distant signal importation on UHF stations on the basis of a proper marginal analysis.

To assess the total impact on UHF of a cable policy that permits distant

---

[9]See Fisher (1964).

signal importation, the status of UHF should be compared in two environments—one in which cable systems import distant signals, and one in which they don't. To be more explicit, suppose that cable penetration without distant signals is estimated at p, and with distant signals at some higher penetration, p'. With distant signals, UHF will have the benefit of cable carriage in a higher fraction of homes ($p' - p$), but will have to compete with distant signals in all p' homes. Without distant signals, the relative amounts of UHF viewing will be p for the cable households and $(1 - h)(p' - p)$ for the $p' - p$ fraction of households that do not subscribe, but would be induced to subscribe by distant signals (where h is the reduction in viewing due to the UHF handicap). If distant signals reduce UHF viewing in cable homes by some fraction f, then the relative amount of UHF viewing with distant signals will be $(1 - f)p'$. UHF stations will therefore be helped by the importation of distant signals if and only if:

$$(1 - f)p' > p + (1 - h)(p' - p) \tag{1}$$

which reduces to

$$p'(h - f) > hp \tag{2}$$

Put another way, the question is whether the elimination of the UHF handicap in the additional homes induced by distant signals to become cable subscribers is worth the increased competition for audience that the UHF station will face in *all* cable homes.

This analytical framework is particularly important, it seems to me, in light of my earlier observations about the effect of distant signal carriage on cable penetration. If distant signals do not lead to a major increase in cable penetration, then it is unlikely that UHF stations would benefit from a cable policy that encouraged distant signal importation. This framework is also useful for examining some of the apparently contradictory information about the UHF handicap. Both NAB and Park, for example, used audience data fom intermixed markets to quantify the UHF handicap. Using data from home counties, NAB concluded that cable would eliminate only part of the UHF handicap; Park, on the basis of total station audiences in 10 markets (and 20 independent data points), concluded that UHF stations could double their audiences in homes where cable eliminated the handicap. Although Park dismisses the differences in these two estimates of the UHF handicap as being due to the very limited data on which the NAB estimate is based, a more complete explanation of the difference must recognize that the two analyses were based on different geographical areas. The NAB analysis considered only audiences in stations' home counties, while Park considered the entire Total Survey Area, which often extends beyond the station's Grade B contour. Recalling Park's identification of the *reception* and *tuning* dimensions of the UHF handicap, it seems reasonable to believe that the tuning problem would not be related to a household's location in a market, but that reception would be considerably less a handicap within a station's home county than in areas beyond the home county. The difference in the NAB and Park estimates of the handicap suggests, therefore, that a major factor in cable's benefit to UHF is the improved reception cable will provide households beyond the metropolitan areas. It is precisely here, however—in the outlying areas—that cable is most likely to succeed *without* distant signals. In terms of Equation (1), I am suggesting that where h is largest (in the outlying areas) the difference $p'-p$ is smallest. As Park's most recent analysis (1971c) shows, penetration increases with the distance of the system from the center of the television market; in fact, his Table 4 predicts that penetration on the edges of a market will be higher *without* distant signals than it will be in the center of the market *with* distant signals.

Effect of Secular Revenue Growth

Another area of significant disagreement among analyses involved in Docket 18397-A concerned how to take into account normal growth through time of industry revenues. Several researchers contended that the loss in station revenue due to audience fractionalization would be made up rather quickly in the course of normal growth of television revenues.[10] Others pointed out that although secular revenue growth has been substantial, the expenses of running a television station have been increasing at the same rate as revenues. To assume, therefore, that normal revenue growth would mitigate the impact of reduced audience levels requires the assumption that expenses will not continue to grow at their historical rate. While expenses may not increase, little analysis was submitted to support this assumption.

The "Compromise Agreement"

The final policy embodied in the FCC's Cable Television Report and Order (1972a) reflected an agreement between broadcasters, the cable industry, and copyright owners. There are two aspects of that agreement, and the subsequent FCC rules, that merit comment in this discussion of the role of analysis in cable policy.

One of the significant differences between the original FCC proposal (1971b) in Chairman Burch's August 5 letter to Senator Pastore and the compromise agreement is the provision in the agreement of exclusivity protection for syndicated programming. These changes were generally viewed as providing significant protection for local broadcasters, but to the best of my knowledge,

---

[10]Park (1971a); Barnett and Greenberg (1969), p. 576.

neither broadcasters nor cable operators had much information on which to base their assessments of the exclusivity rules. Park's recent analysis (1972c)—published seven months after the agreement—is the most thorough investigation of the problem, and I think it is fair to conclude that the decision of the parties to accept this aspect of the proposed compromise was made in a virtual vacuum. Interestingly, Park suggests that the rules will have little effect, but NCTA's comments in FCC Docket 18179 have led some observers to believe that the cable industry now wishes to weaken the exclusivity provisions.

A second change in the compromise agreement was the setting of (apparently) stricter criteria for determining that a signal from outside a market is "significantly viewed" within the market (and hence not to be counted as a distant signal when carried by a cable system). According to the August 5 letter, an independent station was to be considered "significantly viewed" if its average share of audience was at least one percent, and if it was viewed at least once weekly by five percent of the households in the cable system's area; in the compromise agreement, the required minimum audience share was increased to two percent. Because audience data are inevitably estimates based on samples, the FCC had commendably proposed in their August 5 rules that the required audience levels be established with 95 percent confidence. In the final rules, however, the confidence interval was reduced—only one standard deviation was required. Depending on the size of sample used, this reduction has the interesting effect of making the supposedly stricter two percent criterion *easier* to meet than the one percent level. With an effective sample size of 900 or less, it is possible that an estimate of audience share that *would* meet the two percent criterion with the required precision would *not* meet the one percent criterion with the greater precision originally proposed.

This area of the rules is noteworthy for several reasons. First, it is somewhat unusual for a regulatory body to state in its rules specific requirements for statistical precision; to the extent that doing so indicates increased sophistication on the part of policymakers, this is an encouraging development. Second, it is a good example of how subtle (from a research standpoint) some regulatory judgments can become—subtle enough that even most of the parties in Docket 18397-A concerned with the "significant viewing" questions were not aware of the implications of the change. Indeed, the setting of confidence limits required establishing effective sample sizes for the surveys that will be used to estimate audience shares, which leads in turn to complex questions about the statistical efficiency of diary surveys; rating services have only recently begun exploratory research on these questions.

Effect of Analysis on Policy

How much impact did analysis have in Docket 18397-A? As is obvious from my preceding discussion, in some areas I believe the Commission either ignored or did not properly evaluate the evidence before it, but I believe that the decision on distant signal importation was made with more attention to the material that had been submitted than is often the case in policy decisions. If I were to criticize the Commission's handling of the research material, it would be primarily for the failure to make explicit its evaluation of the material. As I have indicated, much of the research was in broad agreement—estimates of audience fractionalization, for example—and presumably in these areas the Commission accepted the results as valid. On other questions—whether normal revenue growth would mitigate audience losses, or would be paralleled by increasing costs—different assumptions led to different conclusions about the impact of policy; in these latter areas, it would have been useful for the Commission to specify what assumptions were made. Although this failure by the Commission to state specific conclusions is both understandable and predictable—as Ken Goodwin has observed, doing so might violate the bureaucratic axiom about always preserving as many options as possible—I don't think that bureaucratic comfort should be a prime criterion in policymaking.

In the final analysis, it seems to me that the principal role of research in Docket 18397-A was to set (or perhaps confirm) limits on policy alternatives. It seems clear that the Commission was committed to allowing the importation of *some* distant signals unless it received overwhelming evidence that to do so would result in severe damage to local television stations. At the same time, I suspect that completely unrestricted carriage of distant signals (or perhaps carriage of four signals) would not have been permitted unless *no* evidence had been submitted indicating that such a policy would damage the television industry.

How Can Analysis Be More Useful?

Before considering *how* analysis can be more effective in policy formulation, it should be noted that there is some question about whether analysis *should* have more influence on policy. Although a great deal of lip service is paid to the need for "better information," "research," etc., it is far from clear that many people at the heart of the policymaking process are terribly interested in elevating the role of analysis in making policy. I find that many attorneys have a tremendous and probably justified cynicism about any kind of research; since many feel that a researcher can always be found who will, for pay, offer proof to support their point of view, it is understandable that they would be reluctant to accord a larger role to research.

Beyond this, there may be another reason for resistance to analysis. Ideally, in policy formulation there should be a clear separation of means and ends—and the goals of policy should not be determined by analysis. This division, however, would require that *explicit decisions* be made about goals, and I have the strong impression that many people in the policymaking process would rather avoid such specific decisions.

For example, it can be argued that cable, while leading to greater diversity, will eventually eliminate much of the very expensive mass-audience programming now done by networks. If this happened television might come to resemble the magazine industry—a great variety of programs would be available through the medium, but television would no longer be a mass medium. (I'm not attempting here to prove that this is the case—let us simply assume for the moment that it is true.) If analysis had convincingly demonstrated this to be the case, a conscious policy decision would have to be made between program diversity and a mass-appeal medium, and I have the distinct impression that most policymakers would not enjoy having to make a deliberate choice between these two alternatives.

Assuming that most of us would like analysis to have an important influence on policy (and let us admit that we have a vested interest in this), how can it be made more effective? I have no answers and only a few suggestions. First, to the extent possible, value judgments that we make as analysts should be made explicit. As obvious and naive as it sounds, I think this is probably most important for analysis that is submitted or sponsored by parties with no apparent vested interest in the policy decision, since such analysis is (quite properly) more likely to be taken at face value. Fortunately, most of the analysis submitted in Docket 18397-A did make explicit whatever value judgments were made; other dockets provide better illustrations of the confusion of analytic and value judgments. Of course, even apparently disinterested parties may not be objective; as former FCC Commissioner Lee Loevinger has pointed out, researchers and academicians develop "vested interests" in their own theories that can be just as strong as the more obvious vested commercial interests of a company or industry.

Second, in situations where considerable amounts of analysis are submitted to a regulatory body, consideration might be given to making (and publishing) a specific evaluation of the material. I believe that such an evaluation was done by the FCC staff in Docket 18937-A, but no formal document was published. Although there are some very competent researchers at the FCC, it may be unreasonable to expect the Commission to have the breadth and depth of expertise to evaluate the volume of material submitted in 18397-A. One way to accomplish this evaluation might be to bring together a group of experts in whatever fields research is submitted for the purpose of reviewing and commenting on the research. The Commission might pose a list of specific questions, and the group would then examine the evidence to determine an answer to each question. What I am suggesting would be analogous, I believe, to a special verdict in a civil suit, in which the panel would make specific findings of fact (which might be that a particular question can't be answered) on the basis of the analysis submitted. The Surgeon General's Scientific Advisory Committee on

Television and Social Behavior, while completely satisfying neither the television industry nor its critics, did demonstrate, I believe, that a group of highly competent researchers was able to reach a consensus in evaluating research evidence on a complex subject. At a much more modest and informal level, I suspect that even a panel of the people who submitted research in 18397-A might have been able to reach an agreement on many issues, and at least made very explicit the areas of disagreement.

Finally, I would like to repeat a comment made at the beginning of this discussion: many of the questions in Docket 18397-A were really quite susceptible to analysis—and future issues will probably be considerably more difficult. Consider, for example, the situation I hypothesized earlier which required a choice between great program diversity and the continuing existence of television as a mass medium. Although this particular choice may never have to be made, I suspect that at some point in time an assessment will be required of the value to the nation of having at least one mass medium of communications—e.g., what would be the social and/or political consequences of *not* having a mass medium. (Presumably this problem won't be answered by economists, but I think we can sympathize with the sociologists and political scientists who may seek to influence policy with their analyses.) This leads me to conclude, then, that it may be a very long time before a Federal Communications Commissioner responds to policy analysts the way Mrs. Sampson responded to Mr. Pratt.

5 The View of an Academic Consultant

William S. Comanor

The economic analysis of policy measures—both those proposed and those already adopted—is a growth industry. Especially in industries subject to regulatory supervision, these studies proliferate until they appear as a necessary accompaniment of regulatory actions. Yet with all the studies carried out, there is a nagging suspicion that they count for relatively little; that the pattern of policy actions would change very little if they had never been undertaken.

Economic studies of specific regulatory matters follow from the nature of the regulatory process. Like most other aspects of the American government, regulatory decisions are taken in an adversary context where it is presumed that the best outcomes flow from the clash of opposing positions. Indeed, the structure of government in this area, as in others, appears designed to promote adversary proceedings. On all sides, the contestants are generally lawyers representing one partial interest or another, and their actions resemble those followed in court proceedings.

In this setting, regulatory officials do not, for the most part, play the role of impartial arbiters but rather of additional contestants in the adversary process. Their powers are constrained not only by the Congress and agencies in the Executive branch of government but also by the courts, and they are often called upon to defend and justify their decisions. Their freedom of action is constrained by existing political support for private interests. Furthermore, regulatory officials come to each decision with a history of past actions behind them and with a set of positions to uphold. In this regard, they are not widely different from the private interests that appear before them. While it is considerably more difficult to specify the objective function of a government agency than that of a private trade association, past actions suggest that the behavior of regulatory commissions departs strongly from what would be indicated by the original regulatory goal of restricting the exercise of monopoly power.[1]

The role of economic studies of regulatory matters follows from the adversary process in which decisions are made. For the most part, these studies are instigated and supported by one of the contending parties. But even where this is not the case, and the analysis comes from sources wholly separate from the contest, the results are *not* widely different. The findings comprise part of

[1] For some discussion of this behavior, see Comanor and Mitchell (1972).

the arsenal of one or a number of the contestants, and the analysis is accepted or rejected as it supports or casts doubt on positions reached on different grounds. In the uses to which policy studies are put, the source of the analysis matters little. Whether directly supported by a contestant or not, the findings are used to provide ammunition for legal briefs and arguments to support positions already reached.

What is suggested above is that analytical studies of regulatory policies are used, for the most part, to defend established positions rather than to assist in determining what these positions will be; that they generally *succeed* rather than *precede* the adoption of positions by the parties concerned.[2] This is not to suggest that details are never altered in response to particular findings but rather that major objectives rarely are.

What often arises in this context are a series of studies dealing with the same general problem area but apparently pointing in very different directions. Although all may be well carried out, little apparent agreement is reached. Rather than providing different answers to the same or similar questions, the studies in fact deal with quite different questions—and for this reason, it may be possible that all are correct on their own terms. It often appears that studies carried out for regulatory processes pass each other as ships in the night, moving in different directions and rarely focusing on the same specific problem.

This characteristic of many studies is especially prevalent because so many are proposed by interested parties. The problem here is not that answers are dictated or consciously slanted in particular directions—although of course this may be so in some cases—but rather that the questions posed often reflect the objectives of the party concerned. The questions originally posed are different, and it is this factor primarily that leads to studies pointing in such varied directions.

When considered in this setting, it is hardly surprising that the role accorded to analytical studies is likely to be low. Such studies take the form, in many instances, of examining or estimating the relationship between specific regulatory measures and one dimension or another of market conduct in the regulated industry. This generalization applies to most of the large number of recent studies dealing with the regulation of cable television. While analytical methods may be highly useful and effective in pointing to the relative merits of alternative roads to the same objective, they are not likely to be as helpful in deciding among alternative objectives—but it is the latter which is often the issue to be decided. The techniques used are largely concerned with the relationships between means and ends—certainly an important and necessary exercise; but they permit individual findings to be written off easily by those who seek different ends. Even where specific findings cannot be rejected, they can be viewed by one adversary or another as not particularly relevant to the question at issue.

As suggested in an earlier paper, regulatory officials often assume the role of

---

[2]Some examples are given in Chapter 10 below.

economic planners of the industry or economic sector for which they have been given responsibility.[3] A consequence of this approach to regulation is that the debate over regulatory actions must be concerned with ultimate planning objectives. Thus, the dictum of "getting cable moving without jeopardizing over-the-air broadcasting" described a search for a compromise solution to the problem of how to structure the television industry. Which of various alternate structures would most secure the planning objectives with which the regulators were concerned?

Regardless of the rhetoric employed, regulatory decisions depend on the relative values placed on ultimate objectives. What benefits should be provided to the public at large and therefore which services deserve the support and protection of the regulatory authorities? How important, for example, is *diversity* in programming as compared with *localism* in program origination and station ownership, and how much should be sacrificed for objectives such as these? In this debate, there is little reliance placed on market outcomes because of an essential unwillingness to accept its dictates as necessarily in the public interest and a fear that desirable new developments will be nipped in the bud by market processes and never permitted to flower and reach their full potential.

Regulatory authorities are concerned with influencing future technology and tastes as well as adjusting to them. What type of industry or economic sector or society is preferred, and to what extent should these choices depend on current consumer preferences as registered in the market place? Whether stated explicitly or not, it is the answers to questions such as these that underlie the choice among objectives, and it is this choice that lies at the heart of the regulatory planning now taking place in the United States. Moreover, it is a choice on which mere analytical results are unlikely to have a major impact.

It seems evident that analytical results are far more likely to influence regulatory decisions where what is at issue is alternate means of achieving the same or similar results. Particularly where some measure of effective costs can be agreed upon, economic studies may indeed indicate that one approach is more efficient than another. Similarly, such studies may be useful in estimating the prospective effects of proposed policy measures. To the extent that relevant questions can be agreed upon, possible answers may well be suggested. Indeed, it is in this context that analytical findings are likely to be most important.

Even where studies focus on specific and agreed-upon objectives, serious obstacles stand in the way to their having an important influence on regulatory decisions. Analytical studies, by their very nature, apply a different standard of proof to those generally applied in legal proceedings. What can often be demonstrated is that a certain response is obtained in, say, nine cases out of ten, or that a high statistical probability exists of this response. What can rarely be demonstrated, on the other hand, is that a particular response is due to a particular event, or that the response is a necessary result of the event. Studies

---

[3]Comanor and Mitchell (1972).

commonly deal with a class of events in which causal relationships are stochastic. Legal proceedings, however, refer to individual events and a deterministic standard of proof is typically required. Even though a statistical relationship between two classes of events may have been found, it can therefore still be argued that there is no evidence that the relationship existed in a particular instance.[4] Although standards of proof are of course not necessarily the same in regulatory as in criminal proceedings, the application of an adversary system in both types of matters does have the effect of reducing the weight given to analytical findings.

Other factors lead to the same conclusion, and they again stem from the adversary context in which analytical results are evaluated and appraised. All such findings inevitably have important qualifications. Theoretical findings are founded on various assumptions that can often be disputed. It can therefore be argued that different findings would have been obtained if only different assumptions had been used. When conflicting results are presented, moreover, the results of all can be more readily ignored. Although conflicting results are surely inevitable in all areas of inquiry, the presence of an adversary system often gives the appearance of conflict even where there is considerable agreement over specific findings. As a result, analytical studies are likely to play a limited role even in circumstances characterized by a high degree of consensus regarding specific findings.

A similar problem exists in the case of quantitative studies. Invariably, arbitrary decisions are made regarding the data and methods employed, and it can therefore always be argued that other decisions could have been made that would have led to different results. Moreover, since it is rarely possible to explore all alternatives, the findings of empirical studies can rarely be accepted without some degree of doubt. While this is true in all circumstances, it is certainly exacerbated by the adversary system. Again, it is difficult to draw conclusions with the degree of assurance generally required in legal proceedings, and it is again easy to cast doubt on findings with which one chooses to disagree.

Indeed, serious doubt must be cast on whether expert findings are really suited to the adversary system. Except in what must be rare cases, it is generally possible to obtain a set of findings to support the position of each advocate. While studies seeking to answer detailed questions are more likely to play a relatively larger role, still the conclusion seems evident that the adversary system by which regulatory decisions are made is largely inconsistent with a strong reliance on analytical results.

---

[4] An example of this form of argument in a different context is that made by representatives of the tobacco industry in challenging the Surgeon General's report on the relationship between cigarette smoking and disease.

6

A View from the Federal Communications Commission[1]

Douglas W. Webbink

In February 1972, the Federal Communications Commission issued its Report and Order on Cable Television (1972a). Previous to making its decision the FCC had received economic studies from its own staff (1970a), from a number of "interested" parties including the National Cable Television Association (done by Comanor and Mitchell, 1970), National Association of Broadcasters (1970, 1971), Association of Maximum Service Telecasters (1970, 1971), American Broadcasting Company (1970, 1971), 21 Television Stations (1970, 1971a), Kaiser Broadcasting Corporation (1970), Hirsch Broadcasting Company (1970), and from a number of "disinterested" parties such as Park (1970, 1971a, 1971c) and Johnson (1970a, 1970b) at The Rand Corporation and McGowan, Noll, and Peck (1971a). The studies varied in quality from sophisticated econometric models to "back-of-envelope" calculations.

Based on the year I spent at the Federal Communications Commission, it is my impression that those studies had very little effect on the FCC decisions. At best, they may have affected slightly some of the Commission's opinions on certain questions (such as the impact of distant signals in certain markets). In most instances they were probably only used to rationalize decisions that had already been made. At worst, they were ignored when they did not fit the preconceived notion of the Commissioners.

As an example, on January 25, 1971, the FCC issued a Memorandum Opinion and Order (1971a) in which it allowed cable systems to file petitions for waiver of a 1969 rule (FCC, 1969). The 1969 rule had required cable systems with over 3,500 subscribers to do a significant amount of local cablecasting. In the 1971 FCC Memorandum Opinion and Order, the Comanor and Mitchell study was mentioned as providing evidence that small cable systems would be unprofitable if required to undertake local cablecasting. At the same time the FCC document indicated that it did not necessarily accept all the results of the Comanor and Mitchell study. Nevertheless, the FCC reference to the Comanor and Mitchell study would seem to indicate that a particular economic study did significantly influence an FCC decision. In fact, however, even before that study was

---

[1] This paper is a result of the academic year 1970-71, which I spent on the Planning Staff of the Federal Communications Commission as a Brookings Institution Economic Policy Fellow; it was written before I joined the Federal Trade Commission. The opinions expressed are my own and not those of the FCC nor the FTC nor their staffs.

submitted in December 1970, some members of the FCC had come to the opinion that the Commission should never have required cable systems with under 10,000 subscribers to do cablecasting. However, there was a strong feeling that the Commission should not admit publicly that a previously made rule was a mistake. The Comanor and Mitchell study gave the Commission an excuse for doing what it already wanted to do anyway, but through a waiver procedure, rather than through a more obvious direct reversal of an existing rule.

As a further indication of how little impact the economic studies had on the final decision, after just two paragraphs of discussion the February 1972 Report and Order dismisses all the economic studies on the impact of distant signals with the statement:

While the reports and studies have been useful in illuminating the various elements of our policy decisions, we cannot rely on any particular report or study as a sure barometer of the future. We simply point out that there is no consensus, and we do not pretend that we can now forecast precisely how cable will evolve in major markets.[2]

This is one of the few official conclusions reached by the Commission after receiving at least a dozen outside economic studies totaling many hundreds of pages. In addition, a 12-page memorandum comparing those studies was presented to the Commission by the Planning Staff in March 1971. The memorandum pointed out such things as the differences between the Rand study and the Broadcast Bureau staff study and the television industry studies with regard to the "UHF handicap" and how it might be changed by cable, as well as whether UHF stations would be helped or hurt on balance by cable. It also pointed out certain obvious facts on which all the outside studies seemed to agree, such as that network VHF stations in smaller markets would be hurt by the importation of distant signals, and that the television stations in one- and two-station markets would be harmed most by distant signals on cable systems.

In the period from March through June 1971, the Commission considered a number of different possible plans for carriage of distant signals. The Commission was given several memoranda by the Cable Bureau and by the Planning Staff as well as several oral briefings by the Cable Bureau and the Broadcast Bureau. These memoranda and briefings provided the Commission with several different tables listing how many distant signals would be allowed in Washington, D.C., under each alternative plan. However, no new estimate was made of what the impact of each plan would be on local television stations, local viewing patterns, etc. It was obviously assumed that if carriage of four distant signals would have a certain size impact on local stations, three or two distant signals would have a smaller impact. But no one ever estimated how much smaller the impact would be.

When the Commission studied the alternative plans, it evidently never asked

[2]FCC (1972a), paragraphs 69-70.

its staff nor outside parties to make new estimates of the effect of each of the alternative plans. In fact, it seems reasonable to believe that when the Commission issued its Order in February 1972, it still had no estimate of how fast cable systems would grow in the top 100 markets under its new rules, nor how much (if at all) television stations would be harmed by the growth of cable.

In any case, the real problem was that the 1972 decision was made through a series of compromises both inside and outside the Commission. The Commission tried to reconcile conflicting interests of many outside groups including broadcasters, cable system owners, educators, public interest groups, Congress, the Administration, etc. At the same time, the Commission tried to develop a package that would give enough to each individual Commissioner to get his vote. Thus, for example, the open access and channel capacity requirements were included to get Commissioner Johnson's vote; the free educational channels were included to get Commissioner H. Rex Lee's vote; and the provisions banning obscene or indecent programming on the access channels were included to get Commissioner Wiley's vote. Presumably the severe restrictions on distant signals were included to get Commissioner Robert E. Lee's vote (although evidently they weren't severe enough) and Chairman Burch's vote.

Under those circumstances, it is not surprising that the 1972 Commission rules contain a number of distinct and unrelated requirements. In addition, there is little rationale, much less honest explanation, of why specific rules were adopted. For example, why should a federal agency require local cable systems to provide free channels for local government and educational organizations, but not for state or national organizations? Why allow two additional distant signals in the largest markets rather than one or ten? Why use a 35-mile radius as the area of coverage for local television service? Why require minimal two-way communications capability? The answers to such questions are not at all obvious. The rules constitute precisely the sort of package one would expect from a committee decision: something for everyone, but no coherent long-run plan. For that reason, additional specific information on distant signal impact, cable or broadcasting station profits, viewing habits, etc., would not have made much difference in the ultimate outcome.

Furthermore, some basic questions were evidently never raised inside the Commission and certainly not addressed in the final document. For example, nowhere does the Commission document deal with the question of what cable *subscribers* want, what *they* are entitled to, and how much *they* should be forced to pay for services they do not want. In addition, this and earlier Commission documents emphasize the need to protect local television service, and viewers of television stations who cannot or will not be able to subscribe to cable service. However, nowhere does the Commission suggest how much protection those groups are entitled to receive. Should rural viewers be guaranteed the level of service they are now receiving, a minimum of three network signals, the same level of service as urban viewers, or what? The

Commission never expresses its opinion on this kind of question. While the studies by the "disinterested" parties and the cable interests dealt with some of these questions, the studies by the broadcasting interests never considered them, and the FCC never asked the broadcasting groups to do such studies.

Suppose the Commission had attempted to do a more thorough job of analysis before issuing its decision. Suppose, for example, it had tried to make a specific decision about whether the impact of distant signals would be "large" or "small." What could have been done differently or might be done better in the future?

Most of the Commissioners and their personal staff advisers do not have the training to read and understand the better and more sophisticated studies laid before them (such as those by Park and by Comanor and Mitchell). For that reason, studies that do not use a great deal of econometrics and whose conclusions are striking (such as the studies by McGowan, Noll, and Peck and by Leland Johnson) are the kind most likely to be read by decisionmaking people in the agency.

Unlike other regulatory agencies such as the Interstate Commerce Commission, Civil Aeronautics Board, Federal Power Commission, and the Federal Trade Commission, the FCC does not have a Bureau of Economics independent of the operating bureaus, which means that there is insufficient staff to do internal studies or to analyze outside studies such as those submitted on cable. There are few economists in the Research Branch of the Broadcast Bureau and the Economic Studies Division of the Common Carrier Bureau. There are no economists in the Cable Bureau.

Furthermore, the total number of economists in the FCC is far fewer than in other regulatory agencies. For example, the FCC has fewer than ten economists, as compared with over 50 in the Federal Trade Commission, despite the fact that the Federal Trade Commission has a smaller total budget than the FCC.[3]

In addition, in the FCC economists in the Broadcast Bureau are chiefly used to compile statistical data for tables, and economists in the Common Carrier Bureau are mainly used to provide data and testify in common carrier hearing cases. Neither division is normally called upon to do continuing sophisticated long-range research, but rather is used for day-to-day "fire-fighting," or long run case preparation. There is also a Planning Staff in the Chairman's Office, but it is not large enough or specialized enough nor was it intended to do long-range economic studies.[4]

---

[3]For Fiscal Year 1970, the FCC had a budget of $24,562,000 as compared with $20,889,213 for the Federal Trade Commission. FCC, *Program and Financial Plan, Fiscal Year 1972*, September 1970, and Federal Trade Commission, *Annual Report of the Federal Trade Commission* for Fiscal Year 1970, p. 63.

[4]The Planning Staff (along with the Cable Television Bureau and to a lesser extent the Broadcast Bureau) was heavily involved in writing certain parts of the 1972 Commission Cable rules, but it had only a minor impact on the really major economic questions, such as how many distant signals the Commission would allow.

To the extent that the Commissioners accepted the results of any of the economic studies submitted, their principle consideration seemed to be who did the study. In other words, it was a matter of accepting or rejecting on faith particular organizations or researchers. The actual quality of the material presented seemed relatively unimportant. For example, various Commissioners appeared to accept or reject Park's conclusions based on what they thought of Rand and Park or what they thought of the NAB and AMST, rather than on the basis of the actual work done.

The studies of the interested parties (NAB, AMST, NCTA) were in many ways so predictable as to be useless. If the NCTA study was of a far higher quality than the others, it was because it was done by academic economists rather than by a for-profit consulting firm. In any case, the Commissioners and their staff advisers are well aware of the fact that many trade associations and profit-making consulting firms have a reputation for providing any results requested and suppressing any unwanted results. For that reason their work is always highly suspect and subject to strong discount, unless Commissioners want support for their previously determined conclusions.

On the other hand, except in unusual cases of outside sponsorship, parties without direct economic interest cannot ordinarily afford to do sophisticated work. Indeed, it was an important and unusual feature of cable proceedings that Park and Johnson were supported by Rand (ultimately by the Ford and Markle Foundations) and McGowan, Noll, and Peck were supported by Brookings (ultimately by the Sloan and Ford Foundations). As both Kenneth Goodwin and Bruce Owen have suggested in their papers, the studies by Park, Johnson, and McGowan, Noll, and Peck tended to make cable seem more important and respectable, irrespective of whether or not their specific conclusions were believed. Those studies made it impossible for the Commission to ignore the fact that there were important social issues at stake beyond the future profitability of the cable and broadcasting industries.

Suppose the Commission had seriously studied each of the economic studies it received. Suppose, indeed, each author had been given a chance to defend his work against the other studies before the Commission or its staff. Because different studies used different assumptions about such things as the number of distant signals to be allowed, the specific markets to be studied, etc., comparisons of the results would have been very difficult. Such comparisons might have been much easier if the Commission had been willing to pose very specific questions to the various parties (such as, what would be the impact of four distant signals on UHF stations in the 25th, 50th, and 75th markets?). Such specific requests for information would have made it far easier to see points of agreement and disagreement among the various parties. Nevertheless, while it was true that some studies were better done than others, all are potentially subject to professional criticism on questions of assumptions, data selection, and methodology. Unless the Commission had a staff of economists able to evaluate the conflicting results, little would have been accomplished by further debate. In the end, after spending additional resources, the Commission might have been forced to ignore the economic studies anyway.

A more general problem in making economic research useful to a regulatory agency such as the FCC is that economists tend to emphasize efficiency, whereas regulators are far more interested in distribution or equity. Microeconomic theory is usually used by economists to ask questions such as how output can be maximized given a cost constraint, or how consumer satisfaction or utility can be maximized, or how consumer's plus producer's surplus can be maximized given some set of constraints. In the case of benefit-cost analysis, the goal is to maximize the benefit-cost ratio or the stream of net benefits. Implicit in such economic analysis is the assumption that every dollar of output is weighted the same, no matter who receives it, whether producer or consumer, rich or poor, white or black.

Regulators, on the other hand, are very much aware of and interested in the question of who receives what share of the output. In its deliberations on cable, the FCC appeared to be interested not only in the question of distributing profits or outputs between producers and consumers, between rich and poor, and between black and white, but also in other distribution characteristics (urban vs. rural consumers, existing vs. new producers, cable system owners vs. TV station owners, UHF vs. VHF TV station owners, etc.). All of the economic studies submitted to the Commission dealt at least implicitly with some of these issues. The studies by McGowan, Noll, and Peck and by Park and Johnson were particularly aimed at these kinds of tradeoffs. However, none of these dealt with all of the tradeoffs that interested the Commission (although the one by McGowan, Noll, and Peck probably came closest to doing that).

It might have been possible to do benefit-cost analyses of alternative policies in which those distributional aspects were more fully taken into account. Instead of weighting benefits received by each person equally, no matter who received it, benefits might be weighted according to characteristics of the persons receiving them. For example, benefits might be weighted directly or inversely by the income of persons receiving those benefits.

The positive income weighting scheme is used in much benefit-cost analysis of safety features. When benefits are measured by the value of a life saved, and the value of a life is assumed to be equivalent to expected lifetime earnings, saving lives of high income persons receives a greater weight than saving lives of low income persons. Such a weighting scheme may lead to the conclusion, for example, that more money should be spent on airline safety and less on bus or subway safety.

On the other hand, much recent public policy in such areas as health and education has emphasized the need to increase the distribution of benefits to the poor. In that case, it might be appropriate to use benefit-cost analysis in which benefits are weighted inversely with income, so that a dollar given to a family with an income of $3,000 counts far more than a dollar given to a family with an income of $30,000.

Because the FCC has traditionally emphasized certain groups such as the poor and persons in rural areas, it might be appropriate to do benefit-cost analyses in which, for example, a rural person was given twice the weight of an urban person. More relevantly, given the FCC's desire to preserve existing television stations and to slow the growth of new cable systems, perhaps a dollar earned by a television station should be given a weight of say five, and a dollar earned by cable firm a weight of one. This kind of economic analysis would help to make weighting schemes and various tradeoffs explicit rather than implicit. Unfortunately, however, it appears that an agency such as the FCC may be reluctant to make such matters explicit. The study by McGowan, Noll, and Peck provided estimates of the possible surplus from the cable industry that could be used to "bribe" or "buy off" or "subsidize" various interest groups. However, both the FCC and some members of the Sloan Commission (for whom McGowan, Noll, and Peck also did a study) appeared to feel that it was not in good taste to talk about "bribes." Consequently, their suggestions do not appear to have been taken very seriously. The studies done by Park and Johnson were considered "in good taste" but many of their specific conclusions based on economic analysis do not appear to have been accepted by the Commission. Certainly no one at the FCC seems to have believed that direct cash subsidies to television stations was a possible alternative to the policy of indirect subsidies through restrictions on the growth of cable. Yet that sort of trade-off information is precisely what the FCC should have used in making its decision.

It is possible that a larger FCC staff of economists and more specific and detailed requests from the FCC for studies by outside groups would improve the usefulness of such studies. Certainly it would help if attention were given to the Commissioner's own apparent goals, and if a greater effort were made to evaluate the distributional effects of various policies. Nevertheless, the ultimate problem with making economic analysis more useful to the FCC is not a problem of doing studies that are more sophisticated or easier for the layman to understand, nor is it really with asking (and answering) more relevant questions. Rather, the problem is with making the regulatory agency less susceptible to outside pressures from Congress, the Administration, and the industries it regulates. The problem is also one of creating an agency in which rational long-run planning can be done, and in which expedient short-run solutions will not always be adopted.

7

Another View from the Federal Communications Commission[1]

Kenneth R. Goodwin

The FCC Has Become an Instrument for Social Choices as to Whether and Under What Conditions New Technology is to be Utilized

In recent years, the FCC has increasingly and routinely become concerned with determining the terms and conditions under which new technologies and services are to be offered to the public. Of the major matters now pending before the Commission, more than half deal with the accommodation of innovation in new technology and services. Cable television and domestic satellites are the best known recent examples but many other applications have been considered. Interconnection to the telephone network, common carrier data processing, specialized common carriers, instructional television fixed service, microwave ovens, land mobile expansion, paging systems and many other services have been previously accommodated. Many new applications are awaiting FCC action.

In the future the Commission will have to deal with video telephone, satellite-to-home broadcasting, information utilities, and the wired nation concept of extending broadband communications to rural and other non-profitable areas.

The Commission has been widely criticized for delaying the introduction of new services such as cable. Currently, the average time for Commission disposition of a major matter is about 2.7 years. A requirement to obtain Commission action appears to delay from one to six years the use of a new service. It is unknown how many developments have not been introduced because of the perceived delay and cost of obtaining FCC approval. It is fairly clear, however, that the Commission does constitute a serious barrier to the introduction of new services and technology in telecommunications.

At the same time the Commission has become an instrument for making social choices as to whether a new technology or service is to be used and under what terms and conditions. Our society has surely reached a stage where it will not automatically embrace new technologies, at least not without public interest constraints being applied. In cases where Federal funds are involved, such as in

---

[1]This paper has been prepared to stimulate ideas on telecommunications policy and represents the author's views only. It should not be interpreted as reflecting the official position of the Federal Communications Commission or its staff.

the development of the SST, the Congress performs this role. In telecommunications, such as cable, domestic satellites, and video-telephone, the FCC has been given primary responsibility.

The Cable Proceedings Were a Model of
External Participation in FCC Rulemaking

The cable proceedings were noteworthy for the amount of involvement by outside parties. More than 90 filings were made in docket 18397-A alone. Three days of panel discussions were held in which participants as well as Commissioners were able to challenge the statements of other panelists. The demands of public interest groups, particulary the demands for access, were so greatly emphasized that they were virtually impossible to ignore.

Participation by other government agencies was of considerable importance. Filings by the Departments of Justice and Health, Education and Welfare, and the Office of Economic Opportunity strengthened the Commissioners' perception of cable as a broadband communications system rather than a system for moving around broadcast signals.

The objectivity and quality of independent research filings carried considerable weight. Studies by The Rand Corporation (Park, 1970, 1971a) and by McGowan, Noll, and Peck (1971a) were frequently cited and given strong credence because of their objectivity and quality.

High quality studies commissioned by parties at interest, such as the Comanor-Mitchell (1970) study for NCTA were of considerable use also. Because their assumptions and methodologies were clearly stated, not only could the results be used, but the conclusions could be discounted, different assumptions inserted and other useful insights obtained. The utility of this study has been further demonstrated by the subsequent widespread use of the Comanor-Mitchell model by other researchers in cable policy.

Widespread Media Coverage of the Cable Debate
Heightened Expectations That the FCC Would
Act to Encourage Cable Growth

News coverage of the FCC cable proceedings, including feature articles in mass magazines such as *Time, Newsweek*, and *Business Week* gave widespread notice of the potential services of cable technology. The FCC panel discussions were televised nationally by the Public Broadcasting Service. Popular review articles, most notably Smith's "The Wired Nation,"[2] and other more specialized publications spread a growing awareness of the potential importance of cable.

---

[2] Smith (1970).

Additionally the growth of cable service, at a rate of approximately 28 percent per year, exposed large numbers of consumers, including Congressmen and other influential figures, to the advantages offered by cable. The combination of widespread consumer interest and extensive media coverage put the spotlight on the FCC and raised expectations that the Commission would act.

Internal FCC Inputs also were Exceptionally Varied and Extensive

In the typical rulemaking proceeding, the Commission is somewhat at the mercy of the line bureau involved. While copies of filings are sent to each Commissioner, he and his staff assistants rarely have the time to read, and certainly not the time to critically examine, test alternatives, and analyze the implications of the individual filings. Typically, the staff presents digests of comments and a draft representing its recommendations as to what should be done. The burden then shifts to the Commissioners and their assistants if any changes are to be made to the staff proposal.

Although the Cable Bureau provided the basic working document for Commission consideration, in this case there were numerous additional internal inputs. Because cable was an exceptionally important proceeding, and because of the extensive panel discussions and intense lobbying efforts, virtually all points of view were heard by the Commissioners; thus they were better informed and better prepared to make their own proposals than is usually the case.

Individual Commissioners researched and drafted statements of their particular viewpoints. For example, Commissioner Johnson's staff investigated the then current status of the installation of high channel capacity systems to support his proposal for imposing minimum channel capacity requirements.

Henry Geller, the Chairman's Special Assistant for Planning and formerly General Counsel for six years, is strongly oriented to reaching an acceptable compromise among contending parties. He developed a comprehensive proposal for the resolution of the most critical issues in the way that he thought would be most acceptable to the Commission.

The Broadcast Bureau prepared and released for public review a report[3] on the potential impact of cable on revenues of local broadcast stations. This report was the subject of many of the filings in the cable docket.

The Planning Office provided a comprehensive document that listed all the goals that one or more Commissioners had previously articulated, identified the implications or necessary conditions for achieving those goals, and suggested alternatives by which those conditions could be achieved. A sample page from that document follows this page as Exhibit I.

---

[3]FCC (1970a).

Exhibit I

Goals	Implications	Alternatives
Make neighborhood tele-communication possible	1. Requires definition of neighborhood or community	a. Leave service area definition and means of providing neighborhood communication to local franchising authorities. (Give advice such as that suggested by Foundation 70.) b. *Require system to develop plan for meeting FCC guidelines subject to local franchising authority review and certification.* c. Specify procedure for local franchising authority to ascertain adequacy of plans,

	2. Requires technical capability of systems to:
	 – originate
	 – distribute programs to a limited geographical area (neighborhood)
		a. *Leave to local franchising authority as in b above.*
		 b. Set FCC requirements
		   1. Require origination by operator.
		   2. Limit size of systems, i.e., maximum of 50,000 homes.
		   3. Require two-way pick up (remote studio) and switching capability.
		   4. Require local origination studio.
		   5. Require channel capacity adequate to serve each community on large systems (i.e., over 50,000).

	3. Requires 1/2 tape play capability at head end	a. Require. b. *Authorize explicitly—and allow other low cost origination techniques—e.g., "Super 8" Film.* c. Take no position now—start new inquiry.

Exhibit II

GOALS AND OBJECTIVES – CABLE TELEVISION

In past documents and discussions, one or more Commissioners have indicated two types of concern about Cable Television:

(1) those related to the direct realization of the full potential of broadband communications networks for our society, particularly those supplemental to present services.
(2) general concerns and specific consequences indirectly related to cable but nevertheless having great importance in regulatory decisions, most importantly, the impact of cable television upon broadcasting.

Direct Goals and Objectives for Cable

1. Improve and equalize the quality of reception of different broadcast signals, particularly UHF.
2. Provide an alternative to mass appeal programming, both commercially supported and public broadcasting, by making it possible for the viewer to select and purchase the service he desires; including:

   — an expanded pool of programming, made possible by the viewers willingness to pay (requires copyright income to creator)
   — specialized programming for nationwide but specialized tastes and interests (requires interconnection)
   — programming with little or no advertising (pay television)
   — time diversity

3. Provide access to the media adequate for all who want it.
4. Diversify media control (limit concentration of control).
5. Facilitate neighborhood communications and provide additional local origination services where broadcasting is not technically or economically feasible.
6. Provide a distribution system that will permit the development of services in addition to the relay of broadcast signals:

   — specialized educational services
   — facsimile distribution (mail, newspapers, etc.)
   — public service information distribution
       — employment opportunities
       — informed electorate
       — health services

Exhibit II (cont.)

- two way (audience response, polling, etc.)
- high resolution video
  - improved television
  - printed material display
  - educational display (e.g., medical teaching)

7. Control abuse of access (obscenity, false warnings, etc.)
8. Ensure adequate quality of service.
9. Ensure non-discriminatory availability of service (e.g., to poor).
10. Reduce discriminatory pricing or other barriers to competitive entry or utilization or growth of the distribution facilities (e.g., newspaper distribution, cable casting, excessive franchise fees).
11. Limit interference between users (e.g., interference from subscriber owner attachment or two-way input). See Docket 18894.
12. Minimize regulation of content (fairness, equal time, etc.).

Indirect Concerns Relevant to Cable Policy Decisions

1. Efficient spectrum utilization.
2. Long term financing for public television (CATV dividend plan).
3. Provide protection of economic base of educational television stations (non-duplication protection of *Sesame Street*).
4. Minimize excess monopoly profits

- broadcasting
- cable

5. Maintain local services rendered by broadcasting stations.
6. Maintain "free" broadcasting service to those not on cable, at least a minimum amount (i.e., 3+1+1).
7. Prevent siphoning of programs and talent from "free" broadcasting.
8. Promote UHF; make profitable; allow stations to recoup losses, as a matter of equity.
9. Foster informed electorate on state and regional issues (anti-leap-frogging).
10. Protect the investment of CP holders not yet on the air.
11. Limit adverse impact upon FM & AM radio.
12. Avoid taking on regulatory responsibilities beyond reasonable expectations of FCC budgetary resources.
13. Provide copyright royalties to program producers.

The Planning Office Focused Attention
on the Commission's Goals for Cable

Only the goals from that document are shown in Exhibit II, following Exhibit I. These goals are divided into two groups, one related to the direct expectations for cable service, the second related to indirect concerns such as the impact of cable upon broadcasting. These goals were in some cases contradictory or mutually exclusive but each represented a desirable end, all other things being equal.

Some options were simply not considered; for example, there was no serious proposal for national conversion to the wired nation,[4] converting over-the-air broadcasting to wire distribution. There clearly was no chance for such a proposal to be approved; thus it was not seriously proposed. The Planning Office document, however, offered a wide range of choices, served as a check list to avoid overlooking serious concerns, and related decision options back to relevant goals.

As the Commission's deliberations proceeded, the Planning Office, the Broadcast Bureau, and the Cable Bureau prepared numerous analyses of the consequences of various proposals, particularly those for limiting distant signal importation. These were generally presented in the form of tables showing the effect of a proposal on each of the top 100 markets. The decisions that evolved were actually made upon this basis of looking at the consequences on a market-by-market basis.

The Need for Consensus Dictated Concessions to
Accommodate the Strongly Held Views of
Individual Commissioners

There was a strong desire to reach a compromise that could be supported by a majority vote and hopefully a substantial majority. Individual Commissioner's demands, such as Commissioner Johnson's insistence on *free* public access channels and Commissioner H. Lee's demand for at least one free, dedicated access channel for education were agreed upon, even though decisions such as the Commission's previous policy requiring compensation of marginal costs for public broadcast interconnection indicate that a majority of the Commissioners opposed free service in principle.

At the time of the Congressional hearings on cable in July 1971, the proposals which were to appear later in the August 5 letter to Congress were supported by six of the seven Commissioners. At those hearings it seemed clear that if the Commission maintained a united front, it would be exceedingly difficult for the Congress to intervene and overrule the Commission.

---

[4] See Smith (1970).

**However, the Threat of Congressional Intervention
Created Uncertainty and the Industry Compromise
Restricted the Commission's Options**

After the Commission made its views known, in its August 5 letter to Congress, there was a period of uncertainty:

1. as to whether Congress would intervene, and
2. what the FCC should do and what Congress might do about copyright, an issue that had been settled in previous Commission deliberations, but with reservations by some Commissioners.

During the fall of 1971, when the rules were being drafted, Commissioner Houser was replaced by Commissioner Reid, an industry compromise among cable operators, broadcasters, and copyright owners was reached, and the Commission's previous solidarity began to crumble.

Once the industry compromise was accomplished, the Commission was faced with a take-it-or-leave-it package. If the Commission modified the compromise in any serious way, one or more parties would be released from their commitments. However, the existence of the compromise introduced a new element into the FCC's relationship with Congress and drew some attention to the degree of unanimity of the Commission's vote. One point of view was that if the Commission remained strongly united, Congress would not intervene. However, it was not clear that the Commission would remain united. In any case, the Congress was considered likely to intervene unless the industry compromise was accepted. The threat of Congressional intervention has to be recognized as a major constraint in the Commission's decisionmaking[5] and an influence on the ultimate outcome.

The rules promulgated in February 1972 incorporated the industry compromise and were not seriously challenged. Congressional oversight hearings shortly afterward reviewed the Commission's proposals and indicated no strong basis for Congressional intervention. Petitions for reconsideration were disposed of with little major change.

On July 19, 1972, the first dozen certificates of compliance under the new rules were approved by the Commission. This action ended a delay of some six years after the Commission's "freeze" of cable in the top 100 markets in its Second Report and Order in March 1966.

**A Variety of Subjective But Obvious and
Rather Clear Conclusions Can Be Drawn
from the Cable Experience**

1. Public interest intervention does have an effect. Strongly presented and well supported demands, such as the demand for access, have to be accommodated in the rulemaking process.

---

[5]See Noll (1971a), p. 15.

2. Objective analysis helps to define issues, constrain fallacious arguments, expedite discussion, and virtually dispose of some issues or concerns that would be time-consuming at best and prejudicial to the public interest at worst. For example, an early Planning Office writeup that candidly discussed the extent of likely public access abuses and of possible methods of controlling abuses helped reduce Commissioner's concern regarding this problem to the point that it was not made a subject of any lengthy discussion.

3. Certain options are foreclosed from consideration because they are perceived to be politically unfeasible, even though economic analysis might show a radical change to be in the best long-term national interest.

4. Short-term interests tend to predominate over long-term principles. This is true because of the overriding concern for short-term growth and a hope that relative positions will change over time as the new entrant becomes stronger. It was on this basis that the NCTA seemed willing to accept constraints in order to avoid protracted proceedings, to obtain some immediate relief, and to grow to fight on more equal terms in future years.

5. Final resolution is very much a political process, encompassing a certain amount of logrolling, considerable concern over Congressional and possible Court review, accommodation to strongly held positions of individual Commissioners, and accommodation of external interests of both industry and public interest groups.

6. The ultimate outcome, the set of conditions under which the service is to be allowed to operate, is considerably different from what would take place in an unregulated market. In addition to limitations that provide economic protection to vested interests, conditions have been imposed which will make cable's entry into the major markets considerably different than if it responded only to market pressures. Conditions such as local origination, channel capacity, access channels, and minimum technical standards have been imposed not only as an additional burden on cable systems, but as conditions to meet perceived public interest needs.

7. Judged by the criteria of restricting cable signal carriage to protect broadcast service, the Commission's end result is somewhat unbalanced. The greatest amount of early cable growth will be channeled into markets 50 to 100 where television stations are relatively weaker. Very little near term growth is expected in the top 50 markets, where broadcast stations are much better able to withstand the economic impact of fragmentation of their markets, and indeed, stand to obtain additional audience by having their signals carried on distant cable systems.

8. Acceptance of the industry compromise is a classic case of political compromise overriding the application of rational analysis. An excellent paper by McGowan, Noll, and Peck (1971b) indicated that virtually all parties competing for the consumer surplus of cable growth could be satisfied except for the exclusivity demands of copyright owners. This paper was called to the attention of the Commission in a lengthy review by the FCC Planning Staff. Yet

the acceptance of the compromise perpetuated exclusivity as the basic mode for television copyright compensation.

9. The Commission should recognize more clearly that one of its major functions is the accommodation of new technology. It should adopt policies and procedures to expedite the process and to specify its evaluation criteria before receiving proposals. However, public officials are very reluctant to limit their options or commit themselves in advance.

10. The expectations generated by research studies, popular articles and, perhaps most importantly, media coverage of such research is an important factor in precipitating decisions. Press clippings about FCC matters are circulated to all Commissioners and top staff members. In some cases the decisionmakers are more influenced by press reports of research findings than by the research reports themselves.

11. Early research that identifies, articulates, and proposes solutions to policy issues may be totally disregarded in the actual decision, yet have a significant effect in forcing the decisionmaking body to address and resolve public policy issues.

Additional Research Should Be Addressed to Cable Regulatory Problems That Have Not Been Resolved or Even Addressed

There are a number of regulatory issues that were not resolved in the recent FCC proceedings. In part, these issues were not resolved because there was little interest or input provided by outside parties. The issues include:

Patchwork Franchising

Given the wide variation in economic viability of different franchising jurisdictions and the natural proclivity of cable operators to build in the most profitable areas, there is a high degree of certainty that some political jurisdictions are going to be bypassed in a patchwork progression of cable construction.

The FCC has left the determination of franchise service areas to local jurisdictions. Only local officials can make the trade-offs between perceived neighborhoods and necessary economic viability.[6] The boundaries of areas

---

[6]Models for the forecast of construction and operating costs, revenues and financial results have been developed by consulting firms, The Rand Corporation, MITRE, and others. Jeffrey Stamps of Cambridge, Massachusetts has developed a simple-to-use model and one-day training seminar package that is available to franchising jurisdictions at modest cost.

where communications are needed, however, do not necessarily coincide with the jurisdictional boundaries of political franchising authorities. A neighborhood may extend over several small jurisdictions or be only a part of a single large jurisdiction. The commercial cable company applicants rarely have an interest in serving all portions of a jurisdiction. While the FCC has required the extension of service to all parties within a franchise region, it has left the local jurisdiction to determine the franchise boundaries.

An additional aspect of this problem is the very real concern over subsidization of one jurisdiction by another, as it appeared following the Rand design of a system for Dayton, Ohio.[7] As in Dayton, there is serious concern in Boston, Washington, D.C., and other major cities that rate averaging over an entire metropolitan area would result in the high density central city areas subsidizing service to low density, high unit cost suburbs. Black/white rich/poor polarizations frequently exacerbate resolution of the basic engineering/economic problem.

While a political solution has been worked out in Dayton by dividing the city into two franchise districts with one of the systems controlled by local minority interests, no solution has been achieved for an entire metropolitan area composed of disparate franchising jurisdictions.

In Washington, D.C., a pioneering effort by the Council of Governments[8] has resulted in a study and appreciation of the problem. By no means, however, has it developed a solution acceptable to the 26 jurisdictions involved, and extensive construction in Washington promises to be stalled for many years.

Short haul multi-channel microwave systems now on the market are facilitating the interconnection of separate systems. Given the basic standardization of all systems carrying standard television signals, future interconnection appears feasible. While the problem of standardizing channel assignments and other interconnection problems are important, they are being worked on by standardizing committees and appear on the way to resolution. Thus it appears that areas that will be bypassed in the initial installation in a metropolitan area can later be interconnected. However, the problem of dealing with cross-subsidy concerns promises to create protracted delays, of perhaps five years or more, unless more positive steps are taken.

It is not clear what steps would be effective. A blanket requirement by the FCC would compel the poor to subsidize the rich in one area and the reverse in another. In Connecticut, where the state Public Utilities Commission consolidated undesirable (non-profitable) areas with desirable ones in order that the entire population would be served, there has been virtually no construction of cable.

The problem is further complicated by uncertainty as to the role federal and local governments will play as users of cable systems for the delivery of social

---

[7] Johnson et al. (1972).

[8] Atlantic Research Corporation and the Metropolitan Washington Council of Governments (1972).

services and what system configurations will be needed to service their requirements. The previously mentioned study by the Washington Metropolitan Council of Governments was primarily directed at exploring local government uses for cable. It represents a significant step in promising direction, but extensive additional cooperative effort is obviously required.

Realization of Neighborhood Communications Services

The Commission's 1970 Notice of Proposed Rulemaking in Docket 18397-A addressed the problem of how to insure the realization of cable's potential for both origination from and distribution to discrete neighborhoods. It invited comments on whether the Commission should impose limitations upon the size of individual cable systems and the several other ways that this goal can be achieved. A more detailed listing is included in Exhibit I earlier in this paper. There was very little comment filed on this problem. Except for its access channel requirements, the Commission's Report and Order (1972a) is entirely silent as to any disposition of this concern. It has left to local jurisdictions the responsibility to draw franchise service boundaries, require program origination access facilities and require switched distribution to discrete areas such as a school district or an area mutually agreeable to the local authorities and the applicant.

It is obviously preferable for local authorities to determine the best solutions to their unique situations. There is, however, no FCC requirement that they do anything at all. There is nothing in the FCC requirements, for example, that would prohibit a city from giving an exclusive franchise to a single system serving 500,000 or more population with only one access studio and no capability for originating programs from, or providing exclusive signal distribution to, a discrete neighborhood or sub-district within the service area.

Since the Commission has not imposed any requirement for neighborhood service capability, it is entirely up to local authorities to do so. Yet I am aware of only one franchising authority that has attempted this; Arlington, Virginia (a county of some 75,000 homes) has required in its invitation for bids that any applicant demonstrate a capability of distributing separate programming, at least to each of its six school districts. There probably are other examples, but most local jurisdictions are overlooking any requirement to provide this capability. Some reserve capacity exists for the future in the form of extra channels to provide this service, but many communities are failing to require the initial installation of access lines, switching, or other hardware, that may be necessary for the future delivery of neighborhood service capability, and will be very expensive to install after the initial installation has been completed.

Separation of System Operation and Content Control

Numerous filings with the FCC, particularly those in which Sidney Dean has had a hand (the American Civil Liberties Union and Americans for Democratic Action) have stressed that local program origination is ultimately inconsistent with common carrier type operation and the full development of cable services. The obvious solution is to separate cable system operators from control of content. This matter has been dealt with at length by Ralph Lee Smith (1970) and other articles.

So far the Commission appears to be persuaded that the short term gains of allowing the operator, who is presumed to have the greatest immediate interest in expanding the scope and range of cable services, outweigh the long term potential danger of conflicts of interest on the part of operators.

Trade press reports of the expected content of the forthcoming report of the President's Committee on Cable Television[9] suggest that it will be strongly oriented to separating operation from content control in order to reduce the need for limitations on cable system ownership.

Its expected legislative proposal may precipitate a decision. It is not clear, however, whether a "pure" separation is essential. If the revenues to be gained from leasing access channels exceed the benefits of excluding competing programming, it may prove acceptable to "grandfather" continuation of operator programming of one or a relatively small number of channels.

Monopoly Regulation of Cable

Cable promises to be a very important, potentially essential, monopoly service. The fundamental issue that the Commission has refused to address is whether cable systems should ultimately become common carriers. It appears to avoid the issue because of a mental association between common carrier status and rate base regulation.

This association is not necessarily valid. There are common carriers whose rates are not regulated, for example coastal station radio. The virtually universal consensus of the Commission, the cable industry, and various interested parties is that it would be a mistake to apply rate base regulation to cable. There is widespread agreement that rate base regulation is undesirable and that it would inhibit growth and financing and create undesirable incentives.

Yet neither is the public likely to tolerate unconscionably excessive profits from a monopoly service. The current interest in public ownership is essentially directed at recapturing excessive monopoly profits for the public. Other

---

[9]BROADCASTING (1972).

regulatory devices such as escalating franchise fee schedules, recapture rights, requirements for operator support of public interest programming, access facilities, etc., or for reinvestment in system expansion (e.g., installation of two-way), are directed at recapturing for the public the profits of the system in excess of a "fair" return on investment of risk capital.

In my judgment, the effort that is being made by the cable industry in opposing the extension of common carrier regulation to cable would better be devoted to seeking alternatives to rate base regulation that would not inhibit investment in the industry but would meet the legitimate demands of cable users that they not be exploited. To my knowledge, however, there is no one doing research on alternatives to rate base regulation.

If cable does develop into a monopoly service, history would indicate that most of the previous regulatory problems in the telephone industry will occur in cable, as well as a few problems similar to those of the broadcast industry (for example, such matters as achieving responsiveness to local needs and developing an open competitive programming market). Two particularly significant problems will be interconnection and the structure of the cable industry.

There are at least three classes of interconnection decisions that will be necessary:

1. when a subscriber wants to attach his own facsimile printer or other terminal device to a cable system and the system operator refuses, or sets discriminatory terms and conditions for doing so;
2. when a cable system wants access to a terrestrial microwave or satellite system of interconnection;
3. when a new-city developer proposes to wire a new community with an integrated broadband/telephone communications system and seeks access to the switched telephone network.

Conclusion

I will not dwell further on the above problems nor on other equally difficult problems (such as how national and local governments and user groups must plan and coordinate their efforts to utilize the capabilities of cable or the potential threat of cable as an invasion of privacy). I have discussed only a few problems which require further research to identify, articulate and force consideration of policy issues. In the matter of regulating cable communications "We've only just begun" and the contribution of additional analysis is badly needed.

8 A Bayesian Framework for Thinking about the Role of Analysis

Rolla Edward Park

One of the central issues in the lengthy FCC proceedings on cable television was the impact that cable might have on over-the-air broadcasting. Cable carrying distant signals will fragment local stations' audiences and tend to reduce their advertising revenues. This may force some stations off the air and make others cut back on the quantity and quality of programming. Thus people who don't subscribe to cable may have their television service reduced—a cost to society that must be balanced against the potential benefits of cable.

Of particular concern to the FCC was the possible impact of cable on nonnetwork (independent) UHF stations. For one thing, nearly all of these stations are in poor financial straits (only 5 out of 48 reported a profit in 1970) and so may be particularly likely to stop broadcasting if their revenues are reduced. For another, the FCC has a firm historical commitment to promote UHF broadcasting as the preferred method to increase the number of television signals available in any locality.

In this note, I am concerned with the evolution of the Commission's views[1] about the likely impact of cable growth on independent UHF television stations. In particular, I should like to know how much these views changed as a result of analysis. For statements of views before and after analysis, I turn to the Commission's own language.

At the opening of Docket No. 18397-A in June 1970, the FCC was pretty well convinced that the threat of cable to UHF was real and serious:

CATV operating with distant signals can achieve significant penetration figures in the major markets—most probably in the order of 50 percent. . . . We [are] convinced that a penetration of this order could pose a real threat to UHF development and that the unfair competition would be significant.[2]

During the next several months (July 1970 through February 1971) a number of analyses of this subject were submitted to the Commission. An FCC staff study[3] pointed out that cable puts UHF stations on the same technical footing

---

[1] Really, of course, only Commissioners have views, not Commissions. "Commission's views" is just convenient shorthand for "views stated in documents adopted by the Commission"—presumably an indication of some sort of the central tendency of the views of individual Commissioners.

[2] FCC (1968). This view is referred to and reaffirmed in FCC (1970b).

[3] FCC (1970a).

as VHF stations by overcoming a number of reception and tuning problems peculiar to UHF. This technical help would tend to offset the harm caused by audience fragmentation. Research done at Rand[4] concluded that for UHF independents the technical help would dominate audience fragmentation, so that cable would actually *increase* these stations' revenues by about 20 percent in the mid-1970s. Analyses filed by a number of interested parties[5] criticized the methods and conclusions of the staff study and the Rand reports.

By August 1971, the Commission's views as to the likely impact of cable on UHF had changed considerably from those held before exposure to the analyses mentioned above and related arguments:

Broadcasters argue that any distant signal cable policy will have a disastrous impact on already shaky UHF stations. On the other hand, we have independent studies such as those submitted by The Rand Corporation suggesting that UHF will be likelier helped than hurt by cable—because UHF is still handicapped by reception problems, and these problems disappear with carriage on cable. Our own study of the matter has persuaded us that it would be wrong to halt cable development on the basis of conjectures as to its impact on UHF stations. We believe the improvements that cable will make in clearer UHF coverage will at least offset the inroads on UHF audiences made by the limited number of distant signals that our rules would permit to be carried.[6]

Did the analyses filed with the Commission bring about this change in views? This question is impossible to answer with certainty, but I shall argue that a "yes" answer is plausible. To do so, I'll use a simple Bayesian model to explain the change in FCC views.

Bayesian statistical theory provides formal methods for making adjustments in probabilistic views as new evidence comes in. In the abstract, the Bayesian framework is as follows: Say you are interested in which of n mutually exclusive, exhaustive alternatives, A_i, $i = 1, \ldots n$, is true. Even before performing an experiment designed to shed some light on the question, you have some idea about how probable the different alternatives are. These prior probabilities, $P(A_i \mid H)$, are based on the background information H that you have before you do the experiment.

You perform the experiment and find that the outcome is X. You know how probable X is if each of the alternatives is true. That is, you know $P(X \mid A_i, H)$. Then Bayes Theorem gives you a way (in fact, the *only* consistent way) to calculate posterior probabilities for the alternatives, that is, probabilities given the way the experiment turned out:

---

[4]Park (1970, 1971a).

[5]National Association of Broadcasters (1970, 1971), the Association of Maximum Service Telecasters (1970, 1971), Twenty-one Television Stations (1970, 1971a), the American Broadcasting Company (1970, 1971), and Kaiser Broadcasting Corporation (1970).

[6]FCC (1971b). A similar statement accompanies the rules finally adopted in FCC (1972a).

$$P(A_i \mid X,H) = \frac{P(A_i \mid H)P(X \mid A_i,H)}{\sum P(A_i \mid H)P(X \mid A_i,H)}$$

Applying this framework to the evolution of the FCC's views on the impact of cable on UHF, I assume that the Commission's views were modified first after receipt of the staff study and the Rand reports, then modified again after receipt of the critical analyses done by the various interested parties. The actual chronology was much more complicated than that, but it doesn't matter.

The three alternatives (A_i) are:

1. helps: cable will significantly help independent UHF stations;
2. neutral: cable will not affect independent UHF stations very much one way or the other;
3. hurts: cable will significantly hurt independent UHF stations.

Prior to receipt of any of the analyses filed in Docket No. 18397-A, the Commission's views were as given in the first quotation above. A reasonable translation of these views into numerical probabilities for our three alternatives is shown in the second column of this table:

Alternative	Prior	$P(X \mid$ alternative)	Posterior
helps	.1	.9	.32
neutral	.2	.6	.43
hurts	.7	.1	.25

That is, the FCC was pretty sure that cable would hurt UHF; P (hurts) = .7. The other alternatives could not be completely ruled out, though. For one thing, there was still some uncertainty about how many people would actually subscribe to cable in large cities with good over-the-air television service. For another thing, the Commission was already aware that cable improved reception of UHF signals.[7] But the probabilities were thought to be small, say P (helps) = .1 and P (neutral) = .2.

The new observation, X, is the appearance of the staff study and the Rand reports. How did they affect the Commission's views? The question in this framework is not whether the Commission believed them or not, but rather: How probable was the appearance of these reports, if the various alternatives were true? The staff study did not unequivocally support any of the alternatives, so how you answer this question depends largely on what you think about the objectivity and competence of the Rand research.

My own guess is that the Commission's assessment was about as shown in the third column of the table above. If cable really helps UHF, there's a high

[7]See FCC (1970b), paragraph 3.

probability that Rand would be able to figure that out and write a report that says so; $P(X \mid \text{helps}) = .9$. Even if cable doesn't do much for UHF one way or the other, it is not too improbable that the Rand reports would say that it helped. This might be partly because the boundary between the two alternatives is fuzzy and a small miscalculation could slide the conclusion one way or the other. Or it might be because (as some have claimed) Rand has a pro-cable bias. Or there may be a bias in any research in favor of definite, interesting conclusions. So perhaps $P(X \mid \text{neutral}) = .6$. But if cable actually hurts UHF, it does not seem very probable that Rand could be biased enough or incompetent enough to say it helps; $P(X \mid \text{hurts}) = .1$.

Applying Bayes Theorem, we get the posterior probabilities shown in the fourth column of the table above. Note that the FCC is *less* certain about the effect of cable on UHF after considering the staff study and the Rand reports than it was before. Before, the probability of "hurts" was quite high. After, the probability distribution is much flatter. The probability of no significant effect is highest, but none of the alternatives has a probability of over .5.

The posterior probabilities from the table above become the priors for the next stage, which is consideration of the critical analyses submitted by the various interested parties, as shown in the table below.

Alternative	Prior	$P(X \mid \text{alternative})$	Posterior
helps	.32	.90	.31
neutral	.43	.95	.43
hurts	.25	1.00	.26

Here, the new information X is the appearance of the interested parties' criticisms of the staff study and the Rand reports. Everyone involved seems to be pretty well convinced that the criticisms would appear no matter what. The probabilities of X conditional on the alternatives are all high, and only slightly greater if cable really hurts UHF (1.0) than if cable helps UHF (.9).

Applying Bayes Theorem to calculate posterior probabilities, we see that the analyses submitted by the interested parties were too (unconditionally) predictable to have much effect on the Commission's views. This does not mean that the interested parties' efforts were wasted, however. For if the appearance of the studies was predictable, their non-appearance would have been a surprise with considerable information content. In terms of the model, if X is the non-appearance of critical studies by the interested parties, the conditional probabilities of X are complements of those shown in the table: $P(X \mid \text{helps}) = .1$, $P(X \mid \text{neutral}) = .05$, $P(X \mid \text{hurts}) = 0$. (Either the critical studies appear, or they do not appear.) Bayes Theorem then yields posterior probabilities that are largest for helps (.6), while neutral is second most probable (.4), and hurts is out of the running (.0). If the interested parties had not submitted their critical analyses, the change in FCC views would have been much sharper than it actually was.

But the critical analyses were submitted, so the final posterior probabilities are those shown in the fourth column of the table above. These probabilities, calculated in the model, correspond very well to the verbal statement of FCC views in the second (post-analysis) quotation above. The increased uncertainty about the exact outcome, the sharp decrease in probability that UHF would be significantly hurt, and the slight edge given to the probability of no significant impact are all evident in the quotation as well as in the model.

Of course, the Commission did not make calculations using Bayes Theorem any more than a driver deciding whether it is safe to pass solves equations relating distances, speeds, and accelerations. But in both cases, it seems to me, the formal model helps one to understand what it is that underlies the subjective processes that actually take place. And the fact that the model does such a good job of explaining the change in FCC views tends to support my contention that the change resulted from the analyses submitted.

Selling Research to Regulatory Agencies[1]

Roger G. Noll

In the aftermath of almost every major public policy decision that involves economic issues, economists ruefully complain that economic research played essentially no important role in policy formulation, despite its great relevance. The recent cable television debate is no exception, as other papers in this volume attest. Replaying a familiar scenario, most of the economists who contributed to the cable debate express dissatisfaction with the Federal Communications Commission's resolution of the issue, largely on the basis of its economic consequences, and blame the unsatisfactory result on the failure of the regulators to give proper weight to economic analysis and arguments. Many of these economists, and some of the noneconomists who followed the economic analysis during the period in which policy was formulated, have been motivated by their dissatisfaction to engage in considerable soul-searching and self-evaluation to discover where they failed in adequately communicating their ideas. Others have blamed decisionmakers, explaining the apparent failure to influence policy by reference to the oft-expressed view that regulators are concerned only with income distribution and/or the welfare of regulated firms, not with economic efficiency.

I do not share my professional colleagues' dismal view of the impact of the dismal science on decisions by regulatory agencies. Certainly economists and their research results do not determine policy outcomes. But the contention that economic analysis has little or no impact is, in my opinion, ridiculous, although impossible either to refute or to prove short of interviewing all decisionmakers while they are under heavy doses of sodium pentathol. The reasons for my disbelief are two-fold.

1. All of the major parties at interest in debates over any issue of government policies towards business—and the cable proceedings provide no exception—feel compelled to commission expensive economic research projects to buttress their cases. While I have never even visited the University of Chicago, I still have

---

[1]The author is a Senior Fellow at the Brookings Institution. Preparation of this manuscript was supported by the Brookings Studies in the Regulation of Economic Activity through a grant from the Ford Foundation. The views expressed in this paper are the author's, and do not necessarily reflect the views of the trustees, officers, and staff of the Brookings Institution.

enough faith in markets to believe that the National Association of Broadcasters, the National Cable Television Association, and similar organizations are probably engaging in two-sided, mutually beneficial transactions.[2] The behavior of the major interest groups in the cable debate, as well as in the other major issues faced by the FCC in recent years, strongly supports the notion that a competent economic analysis is, like a respectable legal brief and a solid engineering report, an essential component of a successful pleading to a regulatory agency. Conversely, no self-respecting Commissioner can sign on to a finding on an important issue unless it responds to the principal economic studies considered during the deliberations. In the final ruling on cable, all of the major economic studies in the docket were referenced and discussed.

2. Although economists may feel that they inevitably lose the major wars of business policy, they nonetheless often affect the outcome of minor skirmishes and even important battles. In the cable proceedings, for example, economists must be given much of the credit for the adoption (the Rand group, notably Johnson) and the repeal (primarily Comanor and Mitchell, with perhaps an assist from McGowan, Noll, and Peck) of the commercial substitution proposal.[3] Furthermore, beginning with the August Letter of Intent, the FCC adopted as its own the position taken by nearly every economist in the proceedings (none explicitly stated an opposing view) that heavy taxation on cable subscribers was inefficient and inequitable.[4] Even the FCC's final position on distant signal importation is remarkably consistent with the economic models it was offered, although it would be far-fetched to claim a cause-effect relation. The FCC said that it wanted to assure that cable systems in large markets had the maximum number of distant signals that would still require them to provide some other

---

[2]The fees paid by the Bell system to its consultants provide some evidence that the marginal revenue product of economists exceeds zero. Between January 1, 1966 and the spring of 1972, Bell paid approximately $700,000 to Dr. Jules Joskow and his National Economic Research Associates, $150,000 to Professor William Baumol, and $185,000 to Professor James Bonbright for consulting and testifying on matters connected with various AT&T rate hearings. See REVISION OF TARIFF FCC. NO. 260, PRIVATE LINE SERVICE, SERIES 5000 (TELPAK), DOCKET 18128, Hearings before the Federal Communications Commission: Vol. 141, p. 13855; Vol. 130, p. 12593; and Vol. 131, pp. 12781-2, respectively. Of course, equity holders in Bell actually paid only a part of these and other consulting fees, since they are allowable costs in determining the company's revenue requirements. Nevertheless, the thought that Bell, if its behavior was economically rational, estimated that the work of these economists would contribute at least $1,000,000 to the revenues of the Bell system (only then would the benefits of their labors have exceeded the cost) should give pause to those who question the importance of economists in regulatory proceedings.

[3]In 1970, the FCC issued a proposed rule that local stations be permitted to insert their commercials on the signals of distant stations imported by cable television systems. The proposed rule was publicly abandoned a year later in Chairman Burch's statement to the Congressional subcommittees that oversee communications policy.

[4]"The ultimate effect of any revenue raising fee is to level an indirect and regressive tax on cable subscribers. . . ." FCC (1971b), p. 49.

new services in order to be successful. According to the most optimistic forecast, the appropriate number to pick to assure this result was two.[5]

   The best illustration of both of the preceding points is the submission of Comanor and Mitchell. Their impact was substantial, especially in its contribution to the demise of many of the service requirements and tax burdens that the FCC provisionally proposed. Certainly NCTA got a good return on its investment in the Comanor-Mitchell study.

The Theory of the Role of Economic Analysis in Regulatory Decisions

The burden of this paper is to explain how economic analysis enters the decisionmaking process of regulatory agencies, and why two studies of equal technical merit, stylistic clarity, and policy relevance may differ widely in their impact upon regulators. This explanation depends upon a simple conceptual model of the behavior of regulatory agencies. A capsulized version of this model is that a regulatory agency honestly attempts to "serve the public interest," but that the indicator it uses to determine if its decisions are in the public interest is the frequency with which its decisions are appealed to either the courts or the congressional subcommittees that oversee the agency's activities.[6] The likelihood that a group can launch an appeal to a regulatory decision depends upon two factors of relevance here:[7] the "facts" of the case—including economic, legal, and engineering analyses—and the extent to which the group is organized to carry on the battle.
   The agency will look at the facts to seek ways in which it can please everyone, but it will be especially interested in not visiting too great a loss on groups that can force the agency into a protracted legal or political battle over a

[5]The most optimistic estimate of the relationship between cable penetration and distant signal importation was provided by McGowan, Noll, and Peck. According to our model, two imported independent stations would make barely viable a system in a market with three network affiliates, one independent, and one public broadcasting station. Given the other requirements imposed by the FCC—twenty-channel capacity, two-way capability, public access channels, etc.—two imported independents would not be enough to make cable investment profitable even if the most optimistic analysis proved correct, although three imported signals *would* be enough. The final rules add various additional restrictions on the choice of stations that can be imported. These further detract from the effect of importation, but none of the submissions to the FCC dealt with those issues explicitly.

[6]One sentence rarely does justice to a theory. More complete explanations can be found in Noll (1971a) and (1971b, especially Chapter 4).

[7]A third factor that can be important in appealing an agency decision but that is not relevant to this discussion is the procedure followed by the agency in gathering evidence and making rules.

decision unfavorable to their interests. The likelihood that a group will appeal an unfavorable decision increases with its per capita stake in the outcome and with the extent to which it is already organized to represent itself on the issue at hand. As both of these increase, the prospective gains from an appeal rise while the costs fall.

The groups most likely to appeal are usually the industries an agency is set up to regulate. Consequently, the agency will, on balance, give them more than an economist's dispassionate benefit-cost analysis would conclude was deserved. But the agency will not "crawl in bed" with the regulated firms—it will only give them enough so that they are unlikely to find an appeal warranted. Thus, while economists and the users of the regulated service will both see the agency as captured by the regulated industry, the regulators and the regulated will still find themselves in conflict and the latter will regard the rulings of the former as significantly restraining its behavior.

In following a policy of minimizing the chance its decisions will be appealed, an agency will generally grant any represented group what it asks as long as it does not seriously offend some other represented group. Of course, the group must first prove that it is well organized and has the financial commitment to make its case. One way a group can prove this is to spend a substantial amount of money on submissions to the relevant docket, including analyses by economic consultants.

When the interests of the well organized groups conflict, the agency will be interested in the stake of each group in the decision, the extent to which each group's stake can be packaged into a politically and/or legally defensible appeal to an adverse agency decision, and the probability that the group will actually appeal (how well organized the group is and how great its financial commitment). The role of economists here is twofold. As in the previous case, because economists are expensive, to buy a few is to show one's commitment to the issues. But in addition, the analytical contents of the economists' submissions are also important, for they shed light on how much each group *thinks* it has at stake in the issue, and how likely the group is to appeal an adverse decision. Thus, the technical quality of the submission is important only to a point. As long as it is at least good enough to be controversial, then it is plausible that the supporters of the submission really believe the results.

The role of the economist without special interest attachment can still be important in this milieu—in fact, he is only less important insofar as he is not actually paid for by an interest as proof of the intensity of its feelings. The "neutral" economic analysis will affect policy if (1) it shows how someone could be benefited by a particular rule without someone else being damaged (i.e., it identifies a Pareto dominant position) or (2) it provides a credible quantification of a serious damage that a well organized group would suffer if a rule were adopted. Conversely, analysis will be irrelevant to the policy debate if it proposes a change that benefits an unorganized group while seriously damaging an organized one, no matter the magnitude by which the first exceeds the second. Nor will economic analysis have much of an effect if it simply attempts to show that the damage another group fears is *de minimus*, as long as it is credible that the organized group could believe the analysis on which its fears are based, even if the latter analysis is inferior in quality to the former.

Applying the Theory to the Cable Decisions

In the cable proceedings, three groups, because they were very well organized and had much at stake, were a serious threat to appeal the FCC's decisions. These groups were: broadcasters, producers of movies and programs for existing broadcasters, and cable systems that had been established under the very restrictive FCC rules of the past. The last group has two types of members: the "Ma and Pa" companies in areas with few viewing options, which need offer very little service in order to succeed, and the big city companies, such as Sterling and Teleprompter, which compete with a variety of free, over-the-air stations and must, therefore, offer new services to attract customers. These latter companies would be strongly oriented towards new cable services under any regime of regulations on signal importation and program exclusivity. At the other extreme, being essentially unrepresented, were two groups: television viewers who favor the conventional light entertainment fare that now occupies nearly all broadcast time, and the as yet nonexistent entrepreneurs who could earn profits by offering cable in large cities if FCC regulations were more liberal.

At varying stages between the extremes, offering some threat to the FCC in that they are loosely organized and have a significant per capita stake in the cable issue, stood numerous other special interest groups. One is the intellectual community, which views cable as the next best hope, now that commercial and public broadcasting have proven disappointing, of offering "diversity"—i.e., more sophisticated programming that pleases intellectuals. Another is composed of ethnic minorities, who see in cable the opportunity to obtain—at long last—broadcast services catering to their tastes and needs. A third is the segment of the program production industry that produces programming that has largely been rejected by the present movie and television markets—the "underground" film or videotape producer. Fourth, political groups see in cable an opportunity to gain access to the most effective of the mass media to deliver their messages. Finally, state and local governments see cable as another opportunity for taxation and regulation—i.e., as a vehicle for increasing both the revenues of government and the power of government officials.

Several of the economists' proposals and conclusions mentioned earlier in this paper met fates that can be explained by the magnitude of their effect on these interest groups. For instance, commercial substitution was initially seen as

Pareto dominant. Viewers and cable companies could have their additional broadcast options, but local stations and program producers would be protected against audience loss. Then, when the costs were seen to be significant, the proposal became a threat to a well-organized group, the existing cable systems.

The FCC has also behaved as though it believes McGowan-Noll-Peck on the importance of distant signal importation to the success of cable in most large markets, even though the professional consensus says otherwise. This is because a "worst case" assumption is called for if one wants to estimate the stake broadcasters might see in fighting FCC rules. But if one accepts the McGowan-Noll-Peck analysis, one must also conclude with us that the viewers' stake in the cable proceedings dwarfs that of all the others combined. This, however, carried less weight with the FCC—for it is highly unlikely that the viewers' interests (and the measure of them implicit in any conclusion that distant signals are critically important in generating cable subscribers) will be the basis of an appeal of the Commission's rules.

These remarks suggest some clear conclusions along the lines of the title of this paper. To sell research on cable to the FCC, it was necessary to have one of three characteristics: (1) to be at an extreme in estimating the potential threat of a proposal to one of the well represented groups, (2) to point to a Pareto dominant (or nearly so—i.e., involving only relatively small costs to a represented group) direction for policy to take, or (3) to make a proposal that provides great benefits to a well represented group at the expense of a poorly represented one.

Since all of the interests could find support in some economic analysis of minimum quality to be credible as a basis for an appeal of an adverse decision, the absolute quality of a particular submission was not important. Thus, the FCC made no attempt to assess the reliability of differing estimates of the demand for cable services or the effect of cable on broadcasters, for an agency conclusion that one of several conflicting economic analyses was of superior quality and should be the basis for cable policy would surely have given rise to political and legal challenges to the agency's decision.

Where Do We Go from Here?

The preceding analysis should rightly be small comfort to those who claim that regulators, and public decisionmakers generally, give inadequate consideration to economic analysis. The role of the economist outlined above is not the one he would like to play. Although the economist—even if supported by a special interest in a regulatory proceeding—usually believes his analysis to be an objective, reasonably comprehensive attempt to shed light on the policy debate, the argument presented here sees his results being used selectively to support special interest positions in an adversary process in which many important interests are represented poorly or not at all. While economic analysis can be extrememly important in a situation in which "the milieu is distinctly one of special interests,"[8] it is almost certain to be used in a manner the analyst finds disappointing or even offensive.

Short of radically reforming the nature of regulatory agencies, the economist has only one mechanism for increasing his influence on regulatory outcomes: to stir up public debate on the issue before the regulatory agency by "popularizing" his views through the mass media. This creates a new kind of interest-group pressure on the decisionmakers, for their decisions will be scrutinized by something akin to a (highly imperfect) public interest representative—the press—as well as the normal mix of regulated special interests. If the agency does, as hypothesized here, use external reactions (such as court cases and subcommittee hearings) to gauge the extent to which it is serving the "public interest," a spate of public criticism in the press can alter its position in much the same fashion as a political appeal to a Congressional subcommittee or a legal appeal to the courts. In addition, publicity might attract the attention of "public interest" lawyers, who then will offer an additional threat that the agency's decision will be appealed.

I can offer no evidence that a publicity campaign by a dedicated economist would bear fruit in regulatory proceedings since, to my knowledge, such a tactic has never been tried. But the testimony by economists before congressional subcommittees is often designed (successfully) to capture space in the newspaper. While subcommittees are different institutions than regulatory agencies, they have much of the special interest sensitivity of the latter (although for different reasons). And yet the role of economic analysis in subcommittee decisions seems freer of the special interest adversary process.

In any case, the model of regulatory decisionmaking outlined here indicates that economists can influence the terms on which their research is used in the regulatory process only by generating external pressure on the agency. In some cases, the interests of a regulated industry may coincide closely enough with the economist's "objective" analysis so that a ready sponsor is available. But if the unrepresented groups have distinctly different interests than any of the well-represented groups, the economist must generate his own pressure group. The only readily available mechanism for achieving this is the press.

---

[8] Herring (1936), p. 183.

10 Conclusion

Rolla Edward Park

To answer questions about the role of analysis in the formation of cable television regulatory policy, eight different authors have described the view from eight different vantage points. I attempt to sketch a composite view in this concluding chapter.[1] Although the several authors used different approaches and emphasized different aspects, they are in remarkable agreement about the role of analysis. Where several touch on the same point, they almost always agree. Where a specific point is made by only one contributor, that point is generally consistent with the overall picture. In the absence of disagreement, I shall not try to attribute views to specific contributors in the summary view that follows.

The Role of Analysis

One point that emerges very clearly is that analysis was not used in accordance with the classic picture of its role. In the classic picture, analysis is a tool to help decisionmakers decide what course to follow. In some cases, analysis might actually indicate which of a number of alternatives best achieves a stated objective or combination of objectives. In other cases, when the objectives are harder to formalize or to aggregate, analysis predicts the effects of adopting each alternative, and the decisionmaker chooses the alternative that has what seems to him to be the best vector of effects.[2] This classic picture bears little resemblance to the way analysis was used in the cable proceedings.[3]

If the classic view is that analysis is a tool in the hands of the decisionmaker, the picture that emerges in our study is that analysis is a weapon in the hands of the contending parties. Indeed, a large share of the analytical effort in the cable proceedings was funded by financially interested parties and used to support predetermined positions. For example, broadcasters supported studies that

---

[1]Roger Noll's paper, Chapter 9, was not received until after this concluding chapter was completed and thus is not reflected in the "composite" view. Although this chapter draws heavily on the work of the other contributors, they are not responsible for the form it has taken.

[2]For an excellent description of analysis in its classical role, see McKean (1958).

[3]In some of the cases discussed by Rivlin (1971), for example the preparation of income maintenance legislation, analysis *does* seem to have been used in its classical role.

emphasized the adverse impact that cable would have on over-the-air television broadcasting. Cable system owners supported a study that emphasized the high cost to cable systems of the FCC's proposed rules.

But even analyses conducted by organizations with no financial interest in the regulatory outcome were caught up in the contention, and used or attacked by the interested parties depending on whether the analyses supported or undermined the parties' positions. Much of the analytical effort funded by broadcasters, for example, took the form of criticism of the FCC staff study (1970a) and the Rand reports.[4] These nonpartisan[5] reports, whose classic role would have been solely to inform the Commission of some likely effects of proposed policies, instead became targets to be blasted by opposing analysts.

It was not only the parties with a financial interest in the outcome who used analysis as a weapon with which to defend predetermined positions. The FCC itself apparently used the Comanor and Mitchell study (1970) in that way. In an order[6] relaxing the requirement that cable systems with over 3,500 subscribers originate local programs, the Commission cited the study as evidence that origination might be too expensive for many small systems. But even before the Comanor-Mitchell study appeared, some Commissioners had made up their minds that the 3,500 figure was too low. Thus the study served only to justify a position already arrived at.

In another example, an individual Commissioner used analysis to defend a predetermined position. Dissenting from the Cable Television Report and Order, Commissioner Robert E. Lee cited[7] results from my first impact study (1970) that indicate that stations in smaller markets will be seriously hurt by cable. Now, Commissioner Lee has long thought that cable poses a serious threat to broadcasting. It seems almost certain that my work did little or nothing to influence his views, and is cited only because it agrees with a position he already held. As evidence, I note that he both disagreed with and failed to mention two other major results of my study: that cable will harm large-market stations very little, and will actually help UHF independent stations.

Even a nonpartisan analyst may use analysis in this way. Once a study is published, for example Park (1970), the analyst has a vested interest in his results. If his study is attacked, he is not unlikely to prepare a second study, for example Park (1971a), defending the results to which he is already to some extent committed.

Upon reflection, it is clear that the classic view of analysis as a tool in the hands of decisionmakers has to break down in a case like the cable television

[4]Concentrating most heavily on Park (1970).

[5]"Nonpartisan" is perhaps not a very good word here, because *all* participants in the cable proceedings obviously cared about the outcome. For lack of a better word, though, I shall use "nonpartisan" to mean "without *financial* interest in the outcome."

[6]FCC (1971a).

[7]FCC (1972b), p. 5.

rulemaking. There were many parties with strong and often conflicting interests (financial and otherwise) in the outcome. Of course they picked up any weapons they could lay their hands on, including their own analyses and those of others. It is probably only in cases in which distributional considerations are not very important that analysis can remain a tool for decisionmakers and not become a weapon for those with conflicting interests in the outcome.

The fact of strong conflicting interests had two consequences that down-graded analysis from the starring role that it plays in the classical picture. First, by spawning competing analyses, it made it harder to rely on any one as a predictor of the effects of proposed policies. Competing analyses naturally had the effect of emphasizing the difficulty and uncertainty of prediction and tended to obscure areas of agreement.

Second and more fundamental, the real disagreements about objectives, about what would constitute an ideal cable policy, made prediction the smaller part of the job. Even if everyone had agreed on the effects of the FCC's proposed rules, the conflicting interests would have remained. For example, agreement on the effects of a certain number of distant signals would not resolve the conflict between broadcasters (who want fewer than that number) and cable operators (who want more). Analysis can do little or nothing to mediate such differences, and mediation was the central task of the FCC proceedings.

So if analysis was relegated to a supporting role in the cable proceedings, what took its place as the star? The answer must be "compromise." The very real and unavoidable conflicts among parties with different interests were settled by giving everyone some of what he wanted, but not all of it. This is not as crass as it may sound. The interests reflected were not just those of the industries with major financial stakes in the outcome. Also included in the regulations are concessions to a broader public interest as it was expressed in nonpartisan filings and as it was perceived by individual Commissioners. Compromise among views of the contending parties and compromise among views of the individual Commissioners were both important in shaping the final regulations.

Besides "compromise," another key word to characterize the cable regulations is "short-term." The interests reflected in the regulations are largely short-term interests. The regulations themselves were viewed almost as temporary expedients, and certainly as subject to change in the future should strong pressures for change arise. There does not seem to have been any attempt to decide on a preferred long-term future for television and make sure that the regulations facilitated that future. In part this was considered unnecessary, because changes could always be made later. And in part any such attempt was avoided because it might have made it impossible to come up with a viable compromise; after all, it was difficult enough to accommodate *short-term* interests without also taking into account long-term plans.

The fact that the proceedings dealt primarily with short-term considerations did much to downgrade another classic role of analysis: the invention of new alternatives. Alternative policies or goals that were suggested, such as Johnson's (1970a) full copyright liability and Smith's (1970) concept of the wired nation, were considered to be utopian—too remote in time or too much of a change from existing policy—and so were not seriously considered.

Even though analysis did not have a starring role, it still had some effect on the proceedings. Three effects seem to be particularly important.

First, it established a framework for discussion. In the debate about the impact of distant signals, for example, everyone seemed to think in terms of the same model. The debate concerned the magnitude of the factors that everyone acknowledged to be important—cable penetration, audience fragmentation, the UHF handicap, audience-revenue relationships. By providing this common framework, analysis undoubtedly facilitated communication and streamlined the discussion.

Second, scholarly writings over the years have served to make cable respectable and to increase everyone's awareness that it is potentially a very important industry. Steiner (1952) provided the theoretical underpinnings for the hope that cable will greatly increase diversity of programming. Papers by Barnett and Greenberg (for example, 1968) exemplify the attractiveness of cable to economists. Smith (1970) contributed to public awareness of the long-term importance of cable, and the filing of McGowan, Noll, and Peck (1971a) emphasized that even the short-term benefits could be substantial. All of this and related work contributed to the FCC's awareness that the potential benefits of cable growth were large.

Third, the net effect of the analyses of the potential impact of cable on broadcasting was to reduce the Commission's worries on this score. Before the analyses were submitted, the FCC was pretty well convinced that cable would seriously harm UHF stations. After, the expectations were more diffuse, with the most likely outcome thought to be that there would be no really substantial effect on UHF one way or the other. Worries that VHF stations would be badly hurt also seem to have been reduced, at least for stations in the large markets.

By thus affecting perceptions of the potential benefits and costs of cable growth, analysis undoubtedly had some effect on the rules adopted. For is those rules were (inevitably) much more the result of compromise than of analysis, still the compromise was hammered out against a background of perceptions of the likely effects of the policies adopted. By strengthening perceptions of cable's possible benefits and damping fears of its offsetting harms, analysis resulted in a compromise outcome that is (to some unknowable degree) more encouraging to cable growth than it otherwise would have been.

The Detailed Questions

We started with a list of questions about the effect of analysis on the views of participants, how analysis is evaluated, partisan vs. nonpartisan analysis, and how analysis might be made more effective. The general discussion above covers some answers; more follow.

Views of Participants

There appears to be some disagreement in the individual papers concerning how analysis affected the FCC's views about the likely impact of cable on broadcasting. On the one hand, Owen, Park, and Webbink explicitly agree that analysis to some extent quieted the FCC's fears of harmful impact. On the other hand, an overlapping set of contributors (Christensen, Owen, Webbink) cite an FCC statement that "we cannot rely on any particular report or study as a sure barometer of the future . . . There is inherent uncertainty . . ."[8] as evidence that the Commission "dismissed" all the studies.

The paradox is resolved by noting that the Commission's views both before and after analysis were probabilistic. There is indeed inherent uncertainty, and the Commission's views quite rightly mirrored this uncertainty. (In fact, I argue in Chapter 8 that the views were *more* uncertain after receipt of the analyses than they were before.)

But the quoted statement is no more than a truism about the impossibility of predicting the future. In particular, it does not imply that the Commission's views did not change, nor does it imply that the change did not come about because of the analyses. In fact, it is apparent that the Commission attached a smaller probability to serious harmful impact after receiving the analyses than it did before. Intuition, as well as the slightly more formal argument in my Chapter 8, suggests that the analyses were the major cause of the shift in views.

The views of participants other than the FCC may also have been affected to some extent by the analytical filings. The National Cable Television Association, for example, is said to have had lengthy and intensive internal discussions of · what positions they ought to take based on the Comanor-Mitchell study.

My own prior views certainly changed as a result of analysis, my own and others. For example, I began with a working hypothesis that there is no such thing as a UHF handicap, that UHF stations' small audiences could be explained entirely by inferior programming. I chose that working hypothesis because of a bias in favor of the simplest possible explanation—Occam's bias, as it were. The FCC staff study, together with my own work, changed my mind.

Evaluation

The Commissioners apparently did not have the time, the inclination, or the training to read all of the filings in the cable dockets. One hopes that they

---

[8]FCC (1972a), paragraph 70.

looked at least at the summaries and conclusions, but even if they did it seems likely that their main impressions of the analytical filings came from sources other than the filings themselves. One very important source is the trade press (principally *Broadcasting* and *Television Digest*), where the analytical filings received quite extensive coverage. Another source is staff briefings and summaries. But staff members, like the Commissioners, have too many other concerns and too little time to do detailed evaluations. Thus the Commissioners are left with a good picture of *who* did the major studies and *what* their most important conclusions were, but with little understanding of *how* (or how well) the studies were done.

If the FCC is not staffed or motivated to evaluate analytical studies in detail, one might hope that competing analysts would do the job—that the Commission's proceedings would function like scholarly journal publication, that "marketplace of ideas" in which a consensus (or at least a clear understanding of irreducible disagreements) usually emerges after sufficient comment and discussion. Indeed, there was no dearth of criticism, but no consensus emerged, probably because the motives for defending established positions were so much stronger than the motives for reaching agreement.

Partisan vs. Nonpartisan Analysis

It is clear that analyses sponsored by financially interested parties had less effect on FCC views than did analyses by nonpartisan organizations. The results of partisan analyses were too predictable to be influential; everyone knew in advance that they would defend established positions. That is not to say that the partisan studies were a waste of effort, however. If one of the interested parties had failed to produce an expected analytical study, his case would have been weakened by its absence.

Partisan studies had little influence on FCC views partly because the Commission's evaluative efforts were so weak. If evaluation had gone farther beyond questions of who did the research and what the results were, into questions of how the research was done, then the detailed arguments in the partisan studies would have had more of a chance to affect FCC views.

How to Make Analysis More Effective

The seven contributors are in remarkably close agreement when answering questions about the role actually played by analysis in the formation of cable policy. The final question, how to make analysis more effective, must be tougher. Here there is, if not disagreement, at least a certain tension among the various views expressed. I shall discuss in turn suggested changes in analysis, in evaluation, and in the Commission.

Suggested Changes in Analysis

Some of the suggested changes in analysis would narrow its focus, some would broaden it. On the one hand, Comanor and Webbink stress the difficulty of trying to compare the results of studies that are based on different assumptions and that attempt to answer different questions. One way around the difficulty would be for the FCC to request analysts to address specified detailed questions "such as, what would be the impact of four distant signals on UHF stations in the 25th, 50th, and 75th markets?" Besides facilitating comparisons among studies, this has the advantage of concentrating on descriptive (as opposed to prescriptive) questions. When simple objectives are absent, the descriptive questions are much more tractable. One worries, though, that this suggestion would increase the risk that important questions might be overlooked. It sometimes takes considerable time, thought, and analysis just to frame the important questions.

Going in the other direction (broadening the focus), Webbink notes that the FCC is very much concerned with the distribution of costs and benefits of policies it might adopt, and proposes that analysis tackle conditional prescriptive questions such as: If broadcasters' revenues are weighted five times as heavily as cable system revenues, what distant signal policy would maximize aggregate (weighted) revenue? This strikes me as being an interesting exercise, but a difficult one—also, one that is likely to be empty unless the FCC is willing to specify the weights. As Dimling points out, they are not likely to be willing.

Owen would broaden the focus in another way: by analyzing long-term issues that have not yet been dealt with. Goodwin has four specific longer-term issues to suggest. There is perhaps some slight tension between this suggestion and our earlier observation that the FCC has a hard enough time working out short-term solutions to accommodate short-term interests. Studies of long-term issues would run the risk of being ignored because they do not deal with immediately pressing problems. On the other hand, they could help to shape informed public or intellectual opinion, and so have an effect when the issue ripens.

Suggested Changes in Evaluation

A number of suggestions were designed to strengthen the process by which competing analyses are evaluated. Such suggestions were implicit in most of the papers. Explicitly, Webbink suggests a well-staffed Bureau of Economics at the FCC, charged with doing research itself and with evaluating that done by others. Dimling proposes a panel of experts to review submitted analyses and delineate areas of agreement and the nature of irreducible disagreements. Dimling also suggests that evaluation, whether by the staff or by his special panel of experts, be published.

It is hard to argue with the idea that a stronger FCC capability for evaluation would be a good thing. There are, though, two opposite dangers that are probably impossible to avoid completely. If the evaluations were made public, they would be just one more weapon to be wielded or attacked by the contending parties. If they were not published, then there would be no check on the evaluators. Perhaps a reasonable compromise would be to publish the evaluation, but only after the docket is closed. Then the evaluators could be evaluated dispassionately, after the regulatory decision has been made.

Suggested Changes in the Commission

As Webbink points out, any large increase in the effectiveness of analysis probably depends more on changes in the Commission than it does on the kinds of changes discussed above. Tautologically stated, analysis will be more effective when the Commissioners are more receptive to analysis and less receptive to pressure from interested parties. (Is there any other way to state it?)

I'm reminded of a suggestion I made some time ago when Rand contracted to help an organization that operates three metropolitan airports that were then plagued by severe congestion. The contract was for something over $150,000, and the first question we faced was how to spend the money in order to be of maximal help. My suggestion, only half in jest, was to use it to send high officials of that organization back to school to study economics. As it turned out, that would almost certainly have had more effect on the way the airports are operated than our (really quite good) analytical studies did.

For someone who wishes that analysis could have more influence on regulatory decisionmaking, the picture sketched above is rather discouraging. Small increases in influence might result from changes in analysis itself and from strengthening FCC evaluation capabilities. Larger increases would be attainable if it were possible to change the attitudes and training of the Commissioners. But one must remember that the Commission's main job is to mediate conflicting interests—all interests, one hopes, not just financial ones. And for that job, compromise is the star, not analysis.

Appendixes

Appendix A

A Brief History of Cable Television and Its Regulation[1]

In every sense except the geographical, Palm Springs is a suburb of Los Angeles; it looks to Los Angeles for most of its services, and its life-style is patterned on that of Los Angeles. But as far as television is concerned, it is cut off from Los Angeles by a mountain range. There arose, accordingly, a demand in Palm Springs for access to Los Angeles television, and, as usual, there were those who were anxious to fill the demand. An entrepreneur erected, on top of a nearby mountain, an elaborate receiving antenna. He then offered, for a fee, to connect any householder in Palm Springs by means of coaxial cable to his antenna. At once, for a few dollars a month the seven VHF channels and three UHF channels from Los Angeles were at the disposal of anyone in Palm Springs willing to pay the price.

In other areas, the incentive may initially have been different but the consequences were the same. In rural areas the local radio dealer sensed a demand for television that was being stifled in the absence of a television signal. He, too, invested in an elaborate antenna, set on a high point of ground, and strung his cable. His returns were partly in the monthly fee he charged, and partly in sales of television sets.

These were the Community Antenna Television services—CATV—with which cable television began. They were almost without exception small enterprises, conducted locally and providing a purely local service. They provided television where otherwise there would have been no television. They added to the audiences of the television stations they imported, without damaging in any way those stations or any others. There were many such CATV[2] services—by 1960 they were estimated to number 640—but they were of purely local consequence, and left television as a whole unruffled.

While all this was going on, television was growing in a fashion that no one, as recently as ten years earlier, could possibly have predicted. Television had become a predominant feature of the American scene, the primary instrument to which the mass of the population turned for entertainment and information.

---

[1] This is Chapter 3 of the report of the Sloan Commission on Cable Communications (1971), copyright © 1971 by the Sloan Foundation and reprinted by permission.

[2] CATV has become an obsolescent term in that "community antennas" are in decreasing use, least of all in new systems, to bring signals into the head-end. The term, CTV, standing simply for cable television, is much to be preferred.

Cable Invades San Diego

The voracity of the appetite for television proved to be immeasurably greater than anything that FCC allocations could satisfy. And thus the next stage in cable television was reached. Again, the example can be taken from California: this time San Diego.

By any of the criteria that the FCC had adopted in 1952, San Diego was well served. Within the city limits were two VHF stations, one of them affiliated with NBC and the other with CBS, both with antennas on high ground and providing service to the entire area. A few miles away, outside FCC jurisdiction in Mexico, was a third VHF station affiliated with ABC. The three together provided what could certainly be construed as a full diet.

Yet, in 1961 cable television invaded San Diego. The entrepreneurs erected a sophisticated antenna, capable of picking up Los Angeles channels from 100-odd miles away, and for a fee of $5.50 a month after a modest installation charge of $19.95—not always insisted upon and later substantially reduced—offered full Los Angeles service to San Diego viewers. Since San Diego was already receiving the three networks, what was being offered in fact was the four independent stations that served Los Angeles with sports, old moving pictures and reruns of network shows, plus the local Los Angeles services provided by the three network affiliates. That was enough. By the end of the decade, the San Diego system was the largest cable television system in the United States, serving 25,000 subscribers. And all this in a city that provides perhaps more opportunities for non-television recreation than any city in the United States of comparable size.

San Diego demonstrated that three channels are not enough to satisfy an ordinary audience, and that a large part of that audience is willing to pay cash out of pocket for more diversified programming than the three networks by themselves provided. At the same time, other communities with modest channel allocations were demonstrating that the system of cable television was not necessarily limited to what a costly antenna could pick off the air. In various locations, where even the extended radius of reception provided by expensive community antennas was insufficient, enterprising businessmen leased microwave links from American Telephone and Telegraph to lengthen their reach, bringing stations into the community from more than a hundred miles away and retransmitting them to their subscribers by cable. The uneven pattern of the FCC allocation, in short, was being filled in by independently controlled community antennas and where these were insufficient by specially leased microwave links. For the country as a whole, the system had become a mixed radiated and cable system, even though cable was by far the junior partner.

Add Color and Program Origination

Meanwhile, the spread of color television was introducing a new element. Even VHF television signals, unlike radio signals, tend somewhat to bounce off large obstacles rather than bend around them. Thus a tall building reflects the signal, and in doing so acts like a weak transmitter, rebroadcasting the signal at the same frequency as the station from which the signal originates. The result is interference, just as if there were two stations broadcasting in the same region at the same frequency. Because the reflected signal is weak, the interference is not pronounced. On a black-and-white set it is usually barely noticeable, although at worst it produces ghost images. But with color reception, far more sensitive to interference, the result is quite likely to be a quite unsatisfactory picture. In New York City, for example, with its multiplicity of tall buildings and the consequent multiplication of reflected signals, color reception can be very bad indeed.

Here was a new opportunity for the cable television entrepreneur. He was able to offer, in New York, something that radiated television could not always supply: a high quality color picture. Cable television invaded New York, despite the presence of a full complement of VHF channels, and began to attract subscribers. New York City franchises became a prize for which the major cable television companies were anxious to compete.

And quickly, the enterprise took on a new aspect. In New York, unlike elsewhere, what the cable system had to offer was not a new picture but merely a better picture. The inducement was smaller, and in marginal situations clearly not enough. Rather than spend $5.00 a month, most New Yorkers within the franchise area were quite willing to put up with a picture that was slightly less than perfect. Something more was needed.

The something more turned out to be programming that was of high interest, and that was not available either on network television or on independent television. Specifically, the systems within New York City sought out exclusive rights to home games of the local basketball and hockey teams. (As in conventional television before it, the first impact of the new system was made by way of sporting events.) In addition, special programming was provided for the black and Spanish-American enclaves that existed within the franchise area.

Cable origination, as it is called, was not entirely new. Most cable systems, even the smallest CATV systems, conventionally used an otherwise unused channel or two by permitting an open, untended camera to transmit news directly off a ticket, or weather off the faces on an instrumental panel. A few systems transmitted low-cost local programming, usually prepared and performed by amateurs or high school groups; a few had even gone so far as to transmit local amateur athletic events. But what New York provided, for the first time, was programming at the level of over-the-air programming, available to cable subscribers alone. The dependence of the cable upon over-the-air transmission was no longer complete. For a few dollars a month one could buy what the rest of television could not provide: athletic events or neighborhood programming of major interest. In New York today, the growth of cable television is limited for the moment primarily by the ability of the cable operators to lay cable and to merchandise their service. The two systems in operation were serving, by mid-1971, more than 80,000 subscribers.

And with that, the prehistory of cable television (one might call it) has come to an end. It had begun as a substitute for over-the-air television where over-the-air television did not exist. It grew later as a supplement to over-the-air television. Today, it has proved that it can be a complement to over-the-air television, providing services that networks and independent stations do not provide. There is only one stage remaining to it: as a replacement for over-the-air television. It is not impossible that it will some day reach that stage.

Cable and the FCC

As the penetration of cable increased beyond the filling of otherwise empty television space, the Federal Communications Commission found itself obliged to grapple with the problems it was beginning to create. Initially the FCC had taken the view that CATV required no special regulation: it was merely doing what the television system would otherwise be unable to accomplish, and doing it without any noticeable interference with established interests. But as cable television began to make its way into communities that were already served, however minimally by established stations, the FCC became more sensitive to the issues that were being raised.

In particular, the FCC has been sensitive to the threat of cable television to the UHF stations it has licensed, and to which it has been committed as a solution, however imperfect, to the problem of channel scarcity. Over the years that commitment has become extensive, culminating, in 1962, in rules requiring that all television sets be capable of receiving UHF as well as VHF signals. (In the absence of real demand many manufacturers have combined quality VHF capacity with inferior UHF capacity, and the intent of the rules has been in part evaded.) The UHF independent station, struggling for survival, may gain initially when cable penetrates its territory and begins to retransmit the UHF signal in a manner that brings it in more crisply and more readily, but in the end cable becomes one more competitor in a market where UHF is already at a disadvantage.

But even the local VHF station is affected. In a small city with but one VHF station, that station gets all the viewers and collects advertising revenue accordingly. Bring in two network competitors by cable and at once its share of audience diminishes by something approaching two-thirds—and its revenues diminish accordingly.

The FCC felt constrained to act, even though it was not entirely clear that it had the authority to act, and struck at cable television at its weakest point: program access. Almost without exception, cable operators held out as inducement to new subscribers what have come to be called "distant signals"—programs broadcast by stations over the television horizon, and sometimes hundreds of miles away from the cable installations. In 1966, the FCC imposed a ban upon the importation of distant signals into the hundred largest television markets, in which are to be found nearly 87 percent of the American viewing public. The pronouncement of that rule led to a judicial challenge of the FCC's authority to regulate cable; that authority was upheld by the Supreme Court in 1968, in *United States v. Southwestern Cable Company.* The result was a "freeze" in the cable industry, at least in those areas where most Americans live.

In addition, copyright owners of the imported programs, and in particular the motion picture industry, were becoming concerned as cable operators profited from copyrighted material without payment of fee. Existing copyright legislation dates back to 1909, when neither conventional nor cable television needed to be taken into account. Litigation proceeds in circumstances where the outcome is determined by judicial interpretation of outdated legislation; the FCC has urged Congress to provide new legislative guidance, but the entire issue has been caught up in Congressional crossfire and remains unresolved.

As the 1960s came to an end, the FCC began to reflect a new attitude. The broadcast industry was not quite so monolithic in opposition to cable, for some broadcast interests were beginning to venture into cable. As cable spread, its public constituency grew, and frustration with stringent rules on importation of signals was freely made known. The lure of cable grew; people began to talk, and journalists write, of the potential value of cable to towns and cities, of a communications revolution, of a medium which might have an important impact on informational and cultural processes.

By 1968, the FCC was trying to free itself somewhat from the restrictive posture of the past. Most recently, in August 1971, it transmitted in a letter to Congress broad outlines of rules under which the FCC proposes to proceed to govern cable television; among other provisions, those proposed rules open up the top hundred markets for the importation of distant signals. The rules are subject to full discussion by all those concerned, who may appear before the FCC or file comments. The FCC hopes to conclude the process by issuing its definitive rulings by March 1, 1972, a date which it will be hard put to meet and which can be delayed by Congressional intervention. Whatever the rules that may be adopted, their impact will be governed by the resolution of copyright problems, either by judicial decision or by new legislation.

But in any case, there appears to be a general concession that the system is here to stay, and even a general intention to encourage its growth, at least mildly. It is reasonable to believe that cable television has at the very least an amber light ahead of it, and in all likelihood a green light. It is substantially free, or promises to become so, to develop in some degree in accord with its own imperatives.

Shape of the Cable Industry Today

As the system stands today, in the fall of 1971, it is still small and still financially unrewarding, at least as compared to conventional television. But it is by no means insignificant, nor is it entirely without financial resources.

In the ten years preceding January 1, 1971, as illustrated in Figure A-1, the cable television industry grew from 640 systems serving 650,000 subscribers to 2,500 systems serving 4.9 million subscribers; its annual growth in subscribers took place at a compounded rate of 22 percent. These figures include a period, in the late 1960s, when growth was severely inhibited by the entry of the FCC into regulatory activities, most of them inimical to cable television. Even during that period, however, subscribers continued to increase at the rate of 22 percent. At that rate, it might be noted, if it should continue over the decade of the seventies, penetration of the system by 1980 will be in excess of 50 percent.

The months since the beginning of 1971 have seen continued rapid growth, particularly in New York City. As closely as a count can be made, there are now in being 2,750 distinct cable systems. They range in size from small CATV systems serving isolated rural areas to the giants in New York and San Diego. In all, the systems now reach 5.9 million households, or approximately 9 percent of all television households in the United States. What is perhaps more significant, franchise applications have been granted, or are being entertained, in more than half of the top thirty markets in the United States, among them New York, Philadelphia, San Francisco, St. Louis, and Atlanta. Construction is actually in progress in cities, small and large, throughout the country; the National Cable Television Association estimates that new subscribers are being added at the rate of about 80,000 a month.

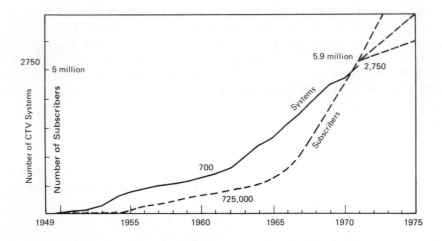

Figure A-1. Historical Growth of Cable Television Systems

Many systems are still what the industry itself calls "Ma and Pa operations," built by local individuals or companies with modest assets and modest goals. Indeed, over the country as a whole the average system has approximately 2,000 subscribers. But in recent years, larger and more substantially financed companies have entered the field; one such company, Teleprompter Corporation, has now more than 600,000 subscribers, or about one-tenth the entire industry. Others are approaching and even threatening to pass that number.

Approximately half the cable systems in the United States are owned or controlled by companies that are otherwise engaged in communications. Over-the-air broadcasters own 30 percent, newspapers and publishers 12 percent, telephone companies 5 percent. One network, the Columbia Broadcasting Company, had extensive interests in cable television before it was obliged by an FCC ruling to divest itself of them.

The cable industry as a whole has not been distinguished by a high level of effort in research and development. The operators themselves do almost none. The industry, moreover, has over its lifetime not been large enough nor well enough financed to encourage research and development on the part of equipment manufacturers; the market was not large enough to support anything more than limited improvements and marginal innovations. To some extent, this deficiency will correct itself, at least as far as immediately perceived needs are concerned, with the growth of cable television.

Over the system as a whole, there is little important origination, although the New York experience is setting a pattern that will certainly be imitated as the remaining top markets are wired. Except in New York subscriptions are still being sold primarily on the basis of additional over-the-air services and a crisper color picture.

There is little interconnection among local systems, and that of minor importance. But there are important stirrings in the field of interconnection. Both COMSAT and Hughes Aircraft Corporation have plans to interconnect by satellite; in the case of Hughes the proposal incorporates plans for program origination.

Commercial interests are becoming progressively more interested in the potential of cable television for the provision of services other than entertainment and information. The same cable that brings ordinary television fare into the home can be used as a conduit to conduct ordinary business: to buy and sell, and to operate in the transfer of payment for merchandise. With some elaboration, it can be arranged to move data of all sorts in and out of the home. The cable, properly arranged, can read meters, serve as a fire and burglar alarm, make market surveys, and even conduct political polls. None of this is fanciful: such services already exist experimentally or are being actively planned.

Finally, as rudimentary as it still is, the system appeals to the American love of gadgets. For a great many people, a few dollars a month is by no means too much to pay for a black box with which the proprietor may divert himself, bringing to his television set something that may be little more in substance, but still more than his neighbor can receive.

In short, there is every sign that cable television, even as it is now constituted, will continue to grow. What the growth can mean to the American people, and how it can be assured, is the substance of [the Sloan Commission] Report.

Appendix B

**Chronology of Federal Regulation of
Cable Television[1]**

April 14, 1959	FCC issued CATV and TV Repeater Services decision. Commission found no basis for asserting authority over CATV systems, and questioned its jurisdiction. 26 FCC 403 (1959)
February 16, 1962	FCC issued the Carter Mountain decision. Commission prohibited a microwave common carrier company from transmitting TV signals via microwave to a CATV system, unless the latter agreed to carriage and non-duplication conditions. Carter Mountain Transmission Corp., 32 FCC 459 (1962), affd., *Carter Mountain Transmission Corp. v. FCC*, 321F. 2d 359, cert denied 375 U.S. 951 (1965)
April 23, 1965	FCC issued First Report and Order Commission asserted jurisdiction over microwave-fed CATV systems, and imposed carriage and non-duplication requirements. 28 FCC 683; Memorandum Opinion and Order, 1 FCC 2d 524
July 28, 1965	FCC's Philadelphia Broadcasting decision. Commission held that CATV systems are not common carriers. Affirmed by *Philadelphia Television Broadcasting Co. v FCC*, 359 F. 2d 282 (1966).
March 8, 1966	FCC issued Second Report and Order. Commission asserted jurisdiction over all CATV systems, required carriage and non-duplication, and specified a hearing before distant signals could be carried in the top 100 markets. 2 FCC 2d 725; C.F.R. 74.1101-1109 (1969)
June 10, 1968	Supreme Court issued Southwestern decision. Stemming from a case in which the FCC halted expansion of a San

---

[1] This chronology was prepared by Henry Geller and Gary Christensen. It was originally published in Coll and Botein (1972), copyright © 1972 by THE NEW YORK LAW JOURNAL, and is reprinted here with minor additions by permission of the authors and the copyright holder.

Diego, Calif., CATV system, the Court found the FCC to have such authority over CATV as is "reasonably ancillary to the effective performance of the Commission's various responsibilities for the regulation of broadcasting."

> *United States v. Southwestern Cable Co.*, 160 nn. 19-22 (1968)

June 17, 1968	Supreme Court issued Fortnightly decision. Court, overturning a lower court ruling, found that CATV systems were not liable for payment of copyright royalties, in a case where there was involved off-the-air Grade B or just beyond Grade B signals.

> *Fortnightly Corp. v. United Artists Television, Inc.*, 392 U.S. 390 (1968)

June 26, 1968

FCC issues 214 decision.

The Commission ruled that Section 214 of the Communications Act requires telephone companies to obtain FCC approval prior to undertaking the construction or extension of CATV lines.

> General Telephone Company of California, 13 FCC 2d 448 (1968), affirmed *General Telephone Co. of Calif. v. FCC*, 413 F. 2d 390 (C.A.D.C.) cert. denied 396 U.S. 888

June 26, 1968

FCC issues leading decision under Second Report. In the Midwest Television decision, the Commission ruled that a San Diego system could not expand further with L.A. signals. *Midwest Television, Inc.*, 13 FCC 2d 478

December 13, 1968

FCC issued Notice of Proposed Rule Making and Inquiry.

Commission closed down hearing process and instituted a proposed "go-no-go" rule based on cable obtaining retransmission consent; also proposed a 3-1 formula for markets 100-on, and anti-leapfrogging provisions. The latter were adopted as interim procedures.

> (Docket No. 18397) 15 FCC 2d 417 (1968). (See also 21 FCC 2d 307 for clarification of retransmission consent.)

October 24, 1969

FCC issued rule requiring CATV origination. Commission permitted all CATV systems to originate their own programming. The FCC also required systems with over

3,500 subscribers to originate programming by April 1, 1971 and allowed all systems to carry advertising at natural breaks.

First Report and Order in Docket 18397, 20 FCC 2d 201 (1969), 23 FCC 2d 825 (1970)

June 25, 1970   FCC issued a series of major rules and rulemaking actions in four areas affecting cable television. Commission proposed a "Public Dividend Plan" which would allow CATV systems to import distant signals subject to specified payment to public broadcasting, deletion of distant commercials, and substitution of commercials of local UHF stations.

Second Report and Order in Docket No. 18397-A. (1) FCC Docket No. 18397-A signal importation proposed rules concern the importation of distant signals from commercial and educational broadcast-television stations, revenue fees and copyright payments, and the use of channels within a single CATV system.

Commercial signals: A CATV system in one of the major television markets would be permitted to bring in four independent (non-network) commercial signals from outside areas. The cable system would substitute commercials from local stations for those on the distant signals. Preference would be given to commercials from local UHF stations, which then could sell advertising on the basis of larger audiences.

Educational signals: A CATV system in a major market could carry the signals of any number of distant non-commercial educational stations if the local educational licensee did not object. At the local educational licensee's request, the CATV operator would run appeals for funds for the local educational station.

Revenues: Major-market CATV systems which import signals from distant commercial or educational stations would pay 5% of their subscription revenues to the Corporation for Public Broadcasting, which would distribute one-half of its share to the local educational station and use the rest for other public broadcasting expenses.

Under these proposed procedures, the FCC says Congress could—and should—pass legislation requiring fair compensation to program copyright owners.

CATV systems outside the Top 100 markets would not be affected by these proposals, except for any copyright payments called for by Congress.

Channel uses: All new CATV systems would be required to have sufficient channel capacity to provide one local origination channel; at least one channel for free use by local governments and for free political broadcasts during campaigns; public access channels for presenting their views on matters of public concern; leased channels for commercial use by third parties; and instructional channels.

Systems with 20 or more channels would have to reserve at least half of them for these purposes.

In any case, remaining channels could be used to carry local and distant television broadcasts and specialized services.

FCC also proposed rules on cross-ownership, federal-state-local regulations, and technical standards.

(2) FCC Docket No. 18891: Ownership Proposed rules contain the Commission's proposals on cross-ownership of CATV systems and other media, and on multiple CATV ownership.

Cross-Ownership: The FCC asked for comments on whether radio stations and CATV systems should be owned by the same person or company within a particular area, and, if so, to what extent. Comments were also invited on shared ownership, or shared use of facilities, between CATV systems and neighborhood or small-community weekly newspapers.

(FCC rules prohibit broadcast-television networks from ownership of CATV systems anywhere; they also ban ownership of a CATV system by a broadcast-television station in the same locality. The question of cross-ownership between daily newspapers and CATV systems is not considered in the FCC's current proposals; the Commission is considering this issue in tandem with a previously proposed rule—Docket 18110—to ban cross-ownership between daily newspapers and broadcast-television stations and between daily newspapers and radio stations.)

The FCC also has asked for comments on whether cross-ownership should be allowed between CATV systems and CATV networks, microwave carriers, CATV-equipment manufacturers, national news magazines, advertising agencies, and other entities whose ownership of CATV systems might not be in the public interest.

Multiple ownership: The Commission has proposed that a single CATV owner be prohibited from having an interest in more than 50 CATV systems of 1,000 or more subscribers each. The limit would be 25 systems if the owner also had an interest in more than one television broadcast station, or more than two AM or FM radio stations, or more than two newspapers. Whatever the limit, the systems would have to be dispersed among markets of various sizes and among the states and multi-state regions.

As an alternative—or as a companion rule—the FCC has proposed that a commonly owned group of CATV systems may serve no more than 2,000,000 subscribers, although subsequent expansion to 2,200,000 would be allowed.

August 5, 1971   FCC sends Letter of Intent to Congress. Proposed comprehensive rules for cable television are spelled out in detail. The proposed rules are in most respects essentially the same as those adopted on February 2, 1972 (see below). The major exception is that they make no provision for exclusivity protection for syndicated programs.

November 8-12, 1971   Compromise agreement among representatives of television broadcasters, cable operators, and copyright owners. The agreement adds exclusivity protection for syndicated programming to the rules proposed by the FCC on August 5, 1971, and makes other less important changes in some of the details of proposed rules.

February 2, 1972   FCC adopted Final Cable Television Decision. New comprehensive rules for regulating cable television were adopted, effective March 31, 1972.

Under the new rules, cable systems in the top 50 markets would be authorized to carry the signals of three full network stations and three independent stations. In television markets from 51 to 100, the standard would be three network signals and two independents, and in markets below 100, systems could carry three full network signals and one independent. If the signals are not available within a 35-mile radius, the systems will be able to import distant signals to reach the required level of service.

Cable systems outside the zones of any TV stations will be able to carry any number of television signals.

Cable systems will be required to carry the closest network affiliates or the closest such station within the same state as the cable system. Independent signals, if they come from the top 25 markets, will have to be from the two closest markets. Systems carrying a third independent signal will be required to choose a UHF station within 200 miles or, if such a station is not available, a VHF signal from the same area or any independent UHF signal. When a program is not available on a regularly carried independent station because of non-duplication protection rules, the cable system may insert a non-protected program from any other station.

The rules provide simultaneous non-duplication protection for local network programming and extensive non-duplication protection for syndicated programs in markets 1-50, with lesser protection in markets 51-100.

CATV systems required to offer the public one "access" channel. Anyone who agreed not to use obscenities, not to advertise or promote a "lottery" would have five free minutes.

CATV operators required to make available a channel for five years at no cost to state and local governments and local educational groups.

New CATV systems required to have a two-way capacity.

CATV systems required to have a minimum capacity of 20 channels in each of the top 100 markets.

Although the Commission rejected licensing of cable systems, prospective cable operators would be required to obtain from the Commission a "certificate of compliance."

CATV operators would also be required to show some machinery for handling complaints, approval of rates at a public hearing, a list of signals carried and an affidavit of service.

Local franchising authorities would be required to pass on cable operator's qualifications, and to set "reasonable deadlines" for construction and operation of cable systems to prevent franchises from remaining inoperative. The Commission said that the local franchising authority would also be required to place a "reasonable limit" on the length of a franchise. Pointing out that a franchise "in perpetuity" would be an "invitation to obsolescence," the Commission suggested 15 years as a maximum franchise term.

The Commission set technical standards to "assure the subscriber at least a minimum standard of reception quality, while at the same time permitting the continuation of technical experimentation." As cablecasting and other cable services are developed, technical standards will be applied in these areas.

February 2, 1972

FCC issued notice of proposed rule making to deal with cable's carriage of sports programming.

The Commission particularly noted the applicability of the Congressional policy in P.L. 87-331 and requested comments on how best to implement that policy.
Docket No. 19417.

March 23, 1972

FCC denies request to stay the rules.
See Memorandum Opinion and Order, FCC 72-270.

Bibliography

Bibliography

American Broadcasting Company, "Comments in FCC Docket No. 18397-A," December 7, 1970.

_____ , "Reply Comments in FCC Docket No. 18397-A," February 10, 1971.

Arkin, Herbert, Letter to Robert D. L'Heureux, General Counsel, National Community Television Association, 1964. Exhibit B for National Community Television Association (1964).

Association of Maximum Service Telecasters, Inc., "Comments in FCC Docket No. 18397-A," December 7, 1970.

_____ , "Reply Comments in FCC Docket No. 18397-A," February 10, 1971.

Atlantic Research Corporation and Metropolitan Washington Council of Governments, "Cable Television for the Washington Metropolitan Area–The Public Service Aspects," May 17, 1972.

Bailey, E.E., and J.C. Malone, "Resource Allocation and the Regulated Firm," BELL JOURNAL OF ECONOMICS AND MANAGEMENT SCIENCE, Vol. 1, spring 1970, pp. 129-142.

Barnett, H.J., and Edward Greenberg, "The Economics of Wired City Television," AMERICAN ECONOMIC REVIEW, June 1968.

_____ , "Regulating CATV Systems: An Analysis of FCC Policy and an Alternative," LAW AND CONTEMPORARY PROBLEMS, Vol. 34, No. 3, 1969.

Barnett, S.R., "Cable Television and Media Concentration," STANFORD LAW REVIEW, January 1970.

_____ , "State, Federal, and Local Regulation of Cable Television," NOTRE DAME LAWYER, April 1972.

BROADCASTING, "Heat's on Cables for Compromise," November 8, 1971a, pp. 16-18.

_____ , "Out of the Trenches for Cable," November 15, 1971b, pp. 16-18.

_____ , "Cable Policy in the Making: Open Entry, Little Control by Government," July 31, 1972, pp. 22-23.

Carter Mountain Transmission Corporation v. FCC, 321F. 2d 359 (D.C. Cir., 1963).

Charles River Associates Incorporated, "The Impact of CATV on Local Television Stations: A Critique of the FCC's Staff Report," September 1970. Appendix C to Twenty-one Television Stations (1970).

Coll, Robert W. (chairman) and Michael Botein (editor), CABLE TELEVISION: TAPPING THE POTENTIAL, The New York Law Journal, New York, 1972.

Comanor, W.S., and B.M. Mitchell, "The Economic Consequences of the Proposed FCC Regulations on the CATV Industry," December 7, 1970. Attachment A to National Cable Television Association (1970). Also appears as Comanor and Mitchell (1971).

Comanor, W.S., and B.M. Mitchell, "Cable Television and the Impact of Regulation," BELL JOURNAL OF ECONOMICS AND MANAGEMENT SCIENCE, Vol. 2, spring 1971, pp. 154-212. Also appears as Comanor and Mitchell (1970).

_____ , "The Cost of Planning: The FCC and Cable Television," JOURNAL OF LAW AND ECONOMICS, Vol. 15, April 1972.

Committee of Copyright Owners, "Reply Comments in FCC Docket No. 18397-A," February 8, 1971.

Dimling, John A., Jr., "Analysis of 'The Economics of the TV-CATV Interface' as it relates to the Impact of Distant Signal Importation on Local Stations," December 7, 1970. Appendix D to National Association of Broadcasters (1970).

Dror, Y., DESIGN FOR POLICY SCIENCE, American Elsevier, New York, 1971.

Federal Communications Commission, FIRST REPORT AND ORDER ON CATV, 38 FCC 683 (1965).

_____ , SECOND REPORT AND ORDER, 2 FCC 2d 725 (1966).

_____ , NOTICE OF PROPOSED RULE MAKING AND NOTICE OF INQUIRY IN DOCKET NO. 18397, FCC 68-1176, 15 FCC 2d 417, 33 Fed. Reg. 19028, 1968.

_____ , FIRST REPORT AND ORDER IN DOCKET NO. 18397, 20 FCC 2d 201, released October 27, 1969.

_____ , "The Economics of the TV-CATV Interface," prepared by the Research Branch, Broadcast Bureau, July 15, 1970a.

_____ , SECOND FURTHER NOTICE OF PROPOSED RULE MAKING IN DOCKET NO. 18397-A, FCC 70-676, 24 FCC 2d 580, 35 Fed. Reg. 11045, 1970b.

_____ , MEMORANDUM OPINION AND ORDER IN DOCKET NO. 18397, FCC 71-78, released January 25, 1971a.

_____ , LETTER OF INTENT: CABLE TELEVISION PROPOSALS, 31 FCC 2d 115, August 5, 1971b.

_____ , CABLE TELEVISION REPORT AND ORDER IN DOCKETS 18397, 18397-A, 18373, 18416, 18892 AND 18894, 37 Fed. Reg. 3252-3341, February 12, 1972a.

_____ , "Cable Television Rules Statements by Commissioners," News Release 82156, February 28, 1972b.

Fischman, Leonard L., "Critique of Study by Rolla Edward Park on Potential Impact of Cable Growth on Television Broadcasting," Economic Research Associates, February 1971a. Appendix A in Twenty-one Television Stations (1971a).

_____ , "Evaluation of FCC August 5, 1971 Distant-Signal Proposals for Cable Television in Terms of Their Impact on Over-the-Air Broadcasting," Economic Associates, Inc., September 1971b. Attachment to Twenty-one Television Stations (1971b).

Fisher, F.M., "The Impact of CATV Competition on Local Television Stations," October 1964. Appendix to National Association of Broadcasters (1964). Summarized in Fisher et al. (1966).

———, and Victor E. Ferrall, Jr., in association with David Belsley and Bridger M. Mitchell, "Community Antenna Television Systems and Local Television Station Audience," QUARTERLY JOURNAL OF ECONOMICS, Vol. 80, No. 2, May 1966, pp. 227-251. Summarizes Fisher (1964).

Herring, E. Pendleton, PUBLIC ADMINISTRATION AND THE PUBLIC INTEREST, McGraw-Hill, New York, 1936.

Hirsch Broadcasting Company, Station KFVS-TV, "Comments in FCC Docket No. 18397-A," September 26, 1970.

Hochberg, P.R., "A Step into the Regulatory Vacuum: Cable Television in the District of Columbia," CATHOLIC UNIVERSITY LAW REVIEW, fall 1971.

Johnson, L.L., THE FUTURE OF CABLE TELEVISION: SOME PROBLEMS OF FEDERAL REGULATION, The Rand Corporation, RM-6199-FF, January 1970a.

———, CABLE TELEVISION AND THE QUESTION OF PROTECTING LOCAL BROADCASTING, The Rand Corporation, R-595-MF, October 1970b.

———, et al., CABLE COMMUNICATIONS IN THE DAYTON MIAMI VALLEY: BASIC REPORT, The Rand Corporation, R-943-KF/FF, January 1972.

Jones, W.K., REGULATION OF CABLE TELEVISION BY THE STATE OF NEW YORK, New York Public Service Commission, December 1970.

Kaiser Broadcasting Corporation, "Comments in FCC Docket No. 18397-A," December 4, 1970.

Kendall, M.G., and A. Stuart, THE ADVANCED THEORY OF STATISTICS, 3rd edition, Griffen, London, 1961.

Kestenbaum, L., "Common Carrier Access to Cable Communications: Regulatory and Economic Issues," prepared for the Sloan Commission on Cable Communications, Sloan Foundation, New York, August 1971.

Lasswell, H.D., A PRE-VIEW OF POLICY SCIENCE, American Elsevier, New York, 1971.

Lindblom, C.E., "The Science of Muddling Through," PUBLIC ADMINISTRATION REVIEW, spring 1959.

McGowan, J.J., R.G. Noll, and M.J. Peck, "Comments Regarding the Public Interest in Commission Rules and Regulations Relating to Cable Television, Signal Importation and the Development of UHF Independent Commercial Stations," submitted to the FCC in Docket No. 18397-A, February 10, 1971a.

———, "Prospects and Policies for CATV," a report prepared for the Sloan Commission on Cable Communications, Sloan Foundation, New York, March 1971b.

McKean, Roland N., EFFICIENCY IN GOVERNMENT THROUGH SYSTEMS ANALYSIS, John Wiley & Sons, New York, 1958.

M.H. Seiden & Associates, Inc., "CATV Distraction Effect," November 1970. Appendix E to Twenty-one Television Stations (1970).

National Association of Broadcasters," Comments in FCC Dockets No. 14895 and 15233," October 1964. Includes Fisher (1964).

_____ , "Comments in FCC Docket No. 18397-A," December 7, 1970. Includes Dimling (1970) and Statistical Research, Inc. (1970).

_____ , "Reply Comments in FCC Docket No. 18397-A," February 10, 1971.

National Cable Television Association, "Comments in FCC Docket No. 18397-A," December 7, 1970. Includes Comanor and Mitchell (1970).

_____ , "Reply Comments in FCC Docket No. 18397-A," February 10, 1971.

National Community Television Association, "Additional Reply Comments in FCC Dockets No. 14895 and 15233," December 14, 1964. Includes Arkin (1964).

Noll, Roger, "The Behavior of Regulatory Agencies," REVIEW OF SOCIAL ECONOMY, Vol. 29, No. 1, March 1971a, pp. 15-19.

_____ , REFORMING REGULATION: AN EVALUATION OF THE ASH COUNCIL PROPOSALS, Brookings, Washington, D.C., 1971b.

Park, R.E., POTENTIAL IMPACT OF CABLE GROWTH ON TELEVISION BROADCASTING, The Rand Corporation, R-587-FF, October 1970. Summarized in Park (1971b).

_____ , CABLE TELEVISION AND UHF BROADCASTING, The Rand Corporation, R-689-MF, January 1971a. Also appears as Park (1972a).

_____ , "The Growth of Cable TV and Its Probable Impact on Over-the-Air Broadcasting," AMERICAN ECONOMIC REVIEW, Vol. 61, No. 2, May 1971b, pp. 69-73. Summarizes Park (1970).

_____ , PROSPECTS FOR CABLE IN THE 100 LARGEST TELEVISION MARKETS, The Rand Corporation, R-875-MF, October 1971c. Also appears as Park (1972b).

_____ , "Cable Television, UHF Broadcasting, and FCC Regulatory Policy," JOURNAL OF LAW AND ECONOMICS, April 1972a. Also appears as Park (1971a).

_____ , "Prospects for Cable in the 100 Largest Television Markets," BELL JOURNAL OF ECONOMICS AND MANAGEMENT SCIENCE, Spring 1972b. Also appears as Park (1971b).

_____ , THE EXCLUSIVITY PROVISIONS OF THE FEDERAL COMMUNICATIONS COMMISSION'S CABLE TELEVISION REGULATIONS, The Rand Corporation, R-1957-FF/MF, June 1972c. Summarized in Park (1972d).

_____ , "After Exclusivity Blackouts, What's Left on the Horizon?" TV COMMUNICATIONS, August 1972d, pp. 46-48. Summarizes Park (1972c).

Pemberton, J., "Foreseeable Problems in a System of Maximum Access," prepared for the Sloan Commission on Cable Communications, Sloan Foundation, New York, May 1971.

Posner, R., "Taxation by Regulation," BELL JOURNAL OF ECONOMICS AND MANAGEMENT SCIENCE, spring 1971.

President's Task Force on Communications Policy, FINAL REPORT, Washington, D.C., 1968a.

————, STAFF PAPERS, Springfield, Va., 1968b.

Rivlin, Alice M., SYSTEMATIC THINKING FOR SOCIAL ACTION, Brookings, Washington, D.C., 1971.

Seiden, Martin H., AN ECONOMIC ANALYSIS OF COMMUNITY ANTENNA TELEVISION SYSTEMS AND THE TELEVISION BROADCASTING INDUSTRY, Washington, D.C., U.S. Government Printing Office, February 12, 1965.

Sloan Commission on Cable Communications, ON THE CABLE: THE TELEVISION OF ABUNDANCE, McGraw-Hill, New York, 1971.

Smith, R.L., "The Wired Nation," THE NATION, May 18, 1970. Also appears in expanded form as Smith (1972).

————, THE WIRED NATION, Harper and Row, New York, 1972. Expanded version of Smith (1970).

Statistical Research, Inc., "The Potential Impact of CATV on Television Stations," fall 1970. Appendix E to National Association of Broadcasters (1970).

Steiner, Peter O., "Program Patterns and Preferences, and the Workability of Competition in Radio Broadcast," QUARTERLY JOURNAL OF ECONOMICS, March 1952, pp. 194-223.

Twenty-one Television Stations, "Comments in FCC Docket No. 18397-A," December 7, 1970. Includes Charles River Associates (1970) and M.H. Seiden & Associates (1970).

————, "Reply Comments in FCC Docket No. 18397-A," February 10, 1971a. Includes Fischman (1971a).

————, "Supplemental Comments in FCC Docket No. 18397-A," October 14, 1971b. Includes Fischman (1971b).

Wells, John D., and Lionel L. Fray (project director), "Comments on the National Cable Television Association's Independent Economic Study," Harbridge House, Inc., Boston, February 8, 1971. Appendix B to Committee of Copyright Owners (1971).

Whitehead, C.T., USES AND LIMITATIONS OF SYSTEMS ANALYSIS, The Rand Corporation, P-3683, September 1967.

Williams, Walter, SOCIAL POLICY RESEARCH AND ANALYSIS: THE EXPERIENCE IN THE FEDERAL SOCIAL AGENCIES, American Elsevier, New York, 1971.

Index

Index

About the Contributors

Gary L. Christensen was General Counsel for the National Cable Television Association during the FCC's cable proceedings. He received his B.S. and LL.B. degrees from the University of South Dakota. He is now a member of the Washington, D.C. law firm of Hogan and Hartson.

William S. Comanor is Associate Professor of Economics, Graduate School of Business, Stanford University. He received his A.B. from Haverford College in 1959 and his Ph. D. from Harvard University in 1964. His recent publications include "Cable Television and the Impact of Regulation," *Bell Journal of Economics and Management Science*, Spring 1971 (with Bridger M. Mitchell), which was prepared with support from the National Cable Television Association and filed in the FCC's cable proceedings, and "The Costs of Planning: The FCC and Cable Television," *The Journal of Law and Economics*, April 1972 (also with Mitchell). He served previously as Special Economic Assistant to the Assistant Attorney General, Antitrust Division, United States Department of Justice.

John A. Dimling, Jr., Vice President and Director of Research for the National Association of Broadcasters (NAB), prepared the analysis of the effects of cable distant signal importation on local television stations which the NAB submitted in the cable proceedings. Prior to joining NAB, he managed the Communications and Systems Research Division, Spindletop Research in Lexington, Kentucky, where his policy-oriented research included studies of the television industry for the President's Task Force on Communications Policy and the Office of Telecommunications Management. In addition to various Spindletop publications, his work has appeared in professional journals. He received an A.B. from Dartmouth College, and an M.S. from Carnegie Mellon University.

Kenneth R. Goodwin is Chief of the Plans and Policy Development Staff of the National Marine Fisheries Service. He established the FCC Planning Staff in the Office of the Chairman in March 1970, and directed it during the two-year period in which the FCC cable policies were developed. He holds a B.S. in physics from Yale University, and, prior to coming to the FCC, was the Bureau of the Budget Examiner responsible for Commerce science and technology activities and the FCC.

Roger G. Noll is a Senior Fellow at the Brookings Institution. Together with John J. McGowan and Merton J. Peck, he filed comments on the public interest in the cable proceedings, work that was sponsored by a Ford Foundation grant. He received his bachelors degree from Caltech, and his masters and doctorate from Harvard. Before joining Brookings, he was on the conomics faculty at Caltech. He is the coauthor (with McGowan and Peck) of a forthcoming book on television regulation.

Bruce M. Owen, a member of the economics faculty at Stanford University, was Chief Economist of the Office of Telecommunications Policy, Executive Office of the President during the period in which the FCC cable policy was developed. He was also a member of the working group of the Cabinet committee on cable television policy appointed by the President in June 1971. He received his B.A. from Williams in 1965, and a Ph.D. from Stanford in 1970. He has published several articles on communication policy issues.

Rolla Edward Park, a senior economist at The Rand Corporation, analyzed the potential impact of cable on broadcasting in reports that were supported by the Ford and Markle Foundations and filed in the FCC cable proceedings. He holds a bachelors degree in engineering from Caltech, a masters in business administration from UCLA, and a doctorate in economics from Princeton. He is the author of numerous reports and articles on communications, transportation and other topics.

Douglas W. Webbink spent the academic year 1970-1971 on the Planning Staff in the Office of the Chairman of the Federal Communications Commission, as a Brookings Institution Economic Policy Fellow. At the FCC he was involved in work on cable which included, among other things, doing a brief analysis of the economic studies filed with the Commission, and an analysis of cable regulatory alternatives. He received a B.A. in physics from Brown University in 1964 and a Ph.D. in economics from Duke University in 1968. From 1967 to 1972 he was on the faculty at the University of North Carolina at Chapel Hill. He is now a senior economist at the Federal Trade Commission. His publications on communications have appeared in professional journals.

Selected Rand Books

Bagdikian, Ben H. THE INFORMATION MACHINES: THEIR IMPACT ON MEN AND THE MEDIA. New York: Harper and Row, 1971.

Bretz, Rudy. A TAXONOMY OF COMMUNICATION MEDIA. Englewood Cliffs, New Jersey: Educational Technology Publications, 1971.

Coleman, James S. and Nancy L. Karweit. INFORMATION SYSTEMS AND PERFORMANCE MEASURES IN SCHOOLS. Englewood Cliffs, New Jersey: Educational Technology Publications, 1972.

Dalkey, Norman C. (ed.) STUDIES IN THE QUALITY OF LIFE: DELPHI AND DECISION-MAKING. Lexington, Mass.: D.C. Heath and Company, 1972.

Dorfman, Robert, Paul A. Samuelson, and Robert M. Solow. LINEAR PROGRAMMING AND ECONOMIC ANALYSIS. New York: McGraw-Hill Book Co., 1958.

Downs, Anthony. INSIDE BUREAUCRACY. Boston, Mass.: Little, Brown and Company, 1967.

Fisher, Gene H. COST CONSIDERATIONS IN SYSTEMS ANALYSIS. New York: American Elsevier Publishing Company, 1971.

Gale, David. THE THEORY OF LINEAR ECONOMIC MODELS. New York: McGraw-Hill Book Company, 1960.

Haggart, Sue A., (ed.) PROGRAM BUDGETING FOR SCHOOL DISTRICT PLANNING. Englewood Cliffs, New Jersey: Educational Technology Publications, 1972.

Hirshleifer, Jack, James C. DeHaven, and Jerome W. Milliman. WATER SUPPLY: ECONOMICS, TECHNOLOGY, AND POLICY. Chicago, Illinois: The University of Chicago, 1960.

Hitch, Charles J. and Roland McKean. THE ECONOMICS OF DEFENSE IN THE NUCLEAR AGE. Cambridge, Mass.: Harvard University Press, 1960.

McKean, Roland N. EFFICIENCY IN GOVERNMENT THROUGH SYSTEMS ANALYSIS: WITH EMPHASIS ON WATER RESOURCE DEVELOPMENT. New York: John Wiley & Sons, Inc., 1958.

Meyer, John R., Martin Wohl, and John F. Kain, THE URBAN TRANSPORTATION PROBLEM. Cambridge, Mass.: Harvard University Press, 1965.

Nelson, Richard R., Merton J. Peck, and Edward D. Kalachek. TECHNOLOGY, ECONOMIC GROWTH AND PUBLIC POLICY. Washington, D.C.: The Brookings Institution, 1967.

Newhouse, Joseph P. and Arthur J. Alexander. AN ECONOMIC ANALYSIS OF PUBLIC LIBRARY SERVICES. Lexington, Mass.: D.C. Heath and Co., 1972.

Novick, David (ed.) PROGRAM BUDGETING: PROGRAM ANALYSIS AND THE FEDERAL BUDGET. Cambridge, Mass.: Harvard University Press, 1965.

Pascal, Anthony. THINKING ABOUT CITIES: NEW PERSPECTIVES ON

URBAN PROBLEMS. Belmont, California: Dickenson Publishing Company, 1970.

Quade, Edward S. and Wayne I. Boucher. SYSTEMS ANALYSIS AND POLICY PLANNING: APPLICATIONS IN DEFENSE. New York: American Elsevier Publishing Company, 1968.

Quade, Edward S. (ed.) ANALYSIS FOR MILITARY DECISIONS. Chicago, Illinois: Rand McNally and Company—Amsterdam, The Netherlands: North-Holland Publishing Company, 1964.

Williams, John D. THE COMPLEAT STRATEGYST: BEING A PRIMER ON THE THEORY OF GAMES OF STRATEGY. New York: McGraw-Hill Book Company, 1954.